MW00581626

Thinking and Being

Thinking and Being

IRAD KIMHI

HARVARD UNIVERSITY PRESS

Cambridge, Massachusetts & London, England / 2018

Copyright © 2018 by the President and Fellows of Harvard College
All rights reserved
Printed in the United States of America

Third printing

Library of Congress Cataloging-in-Publication Data
Names: Kimhi, Irad, author.
Title: Thinking and being / Irad Kimhi.
Description: Cambridge, Massachusetts : Harvard University Press,
    2018. | Includes bibliographical references and index.
Identifiers: LCCN 2017049673 | ISBN 9780674967892 (cloth : alk.
    paper)
Subjects: LCSH: Frege, Gottlob, 1848–1925. | Analysis (Philosophy) |
    Thought and thinking. | Logic. | Ontology. | Language and logic.
Classification: LCC B808.5 .K56 2018 | DDC 128 / .33—dc23
    LC record available at https://lccn.loc.gov/2017049673

Contents

Thinking and Being

Introduction

1. The Gate of Philosophy

It is night.[1] A young man is carried in a glowing chariot by the Daughters of the Sun to the gates of the Ways of Night and Day. There he is welcomed by a nameless goddess who will guide him toward Reality / Truth *(aletheia)*.

This is the opening scene of Parmenides's didactic poem *On Nature*. It is the first work of *philosophy,* where this is to be understood as the logical study of thinking and of what is (being). One can look to this poem for the origin of the very idea of philosophical logic—the idea of a study that achieves a mutual illumination of thinking and what is: an illumination through a clarification of human discursive activity in which truth (reality, *aletheia*) is at stake. Philosophical logic, so understood, is a first-personal engagement from *within* the activity of thinking, one which allows the articulation and comprehension of thinking to emerge from out of itself. The personal, so understood, *is* the logical.[2] It

---

[1] Or maybe not. See, for example, Mitchell Miller, "Ambiguity and Transport: Reflections on the Proem to Parmenides' Poem," *Oxford Studies in Ancient Philosophy* 30 (2006): 18–19.

[2] It is wrong, I shall argue, to dissociate the concern that I have, in doing philosophical logic, with my own thinking, from that which I have with the thinking of others—the thinking of those with whom, for example, I can agree or disagree and from whom I can learn. In particular, it is wrong to dissociate logic as a comprehension and articulation of the activity of the logical "I" from a comprehension of the thinking of the empirical "I."

is the activity of the logical "I"—in a sense of "activity" to be elucidated below.[3]

This book proceeds from the conviction that philosophical logic can make progress only by working through certain puzzles—such as those that come into view only once one is struck by that which is most puzzling in the pronouncements of the goddess who stands at the outset, the gate, of Parmenides's poem.

It has become difficult, in our time, to be struck by that which is most puzzling in these pronouncements. For we are apt to think that we have already put the difficulty behind us. Our misplaced confidence stems from our present conceptions of logic and language. We fail to see that, for all of their technical and mathematical sophistication, these conceptions are inadequate to the task of philosophical logic indicated above.

At the outset, the gate, of Parmenides's poem, the goddess presents the young man with a choice:

> But come now, I will tell you—and you, when you have heard the story, bring it safely away—which are the only routes of inquiry that are for thinking: the one, that is and that it is not possible for it not to be, is the path of Persuasion (for it attends upon Truth); the other, that it is not and that it is right that it not be, this indeed I declare to you to be a path entirely unable to be investigated: For neither can you know what is not (for it is not to be accomplished) nor can you declare it. (Frag. B2)[4]

The choice is between two ways: the way of *esti* ("is") and the way of *ouk esti* ("is not"). We can call them the *positive way* and the *negative way*. The verb *esti* and its negation occur here without a subject or complement. (Greek does not require one.) The poem is usually understood as disclosing through its logical progression the unspecified subject of the *esti*.[5] The goddess guides the

---

[3] This strictly logical or propositional sense of "activity" will need to be carefully distinguished from a variety of nonlogical senses of activity that are associated with the verb.

[4] Patricia Curd, ed., *A Presocratics Reader* (Indianapolis: Hackett, 2001), 55.

[5] Cf. Charles Kahn:

> [I]n thus confronting us with the bare choice between *esti* and its denial, Parmenides is in a way stating the principle of noncontradiction. . . . Now the law of noncontradiction was not formulated explicitly (as far as we know) until Plato's *Republic* (4.436b–437a); and the excluded middle is first recognized as such by Aristotle (*Meta* 4.7). But these principles are

young man toward *the positive way,* which she names *the way of truth,* by arguing that *the negative way* is not genuinely available since it cannot be known or stated.

Competing contemporary readings of this argument correspond to different readings of the Greek verb *to be (esti).* These readings, in turn, reflect a modern philosophical tendency to think that we are well advised to distinguish between various senses of the verb *to be.* One early expression of this tendency is to be found in J. S. Mill's *Logic.* Mill distinguishes two senses or usages of the verb *is:* the first is used to ascribe existence and the second to attach a predicate. Mill complained of a fog that arose from overlooking this ambiguity in the word *is*—a fog that he claimed "diffused itself at an early period over the whole surface of metaphysics."

In his "The Greek Verb 'to Be,' and the Concept of Being," Charles Kahn argues that Mill's distinction (between the existential *is* and the predicative *is*) conflates a grammatical / syntactical distinction with a semantical one. From Kahn's point of view, Mill confuses the distinction between a *complete* (or absolute or one-place) use of "is" (which is not complemented by a predicate) and an *incomplete* (or predicative or two-place) use of is, with a further distinction between existential and predicative senses of the copula. Kahn thinks that Mill thereby overlooks a nonexistential employment of the complete copula—one that Kahn takes to express the *veridical* sense of the verb *to be;* in its veridical sense "is" means *to be true* or *to be the case.* With the foregrounding of this sense of the verb, Kahn maintains, philosophy first emerges in ancient Greece.

Implicit in the talk of a veridical sense of the verb *to be* is a notion of beings that have propositional complexity—veridical beings. Kahn assumes that the veridical sense of the expression is a complete propositional verb—a verb that takes a propositionally structured item as its subject: a content clause or a sentence. Kahn further assumes that the intrinsic being of such propositionally structured items is separable from their veridical being, namely, that they exist independently of being true, namely, the veridical use of "to be" is in no way existential.

---

here on the tip of Parmenides' tongue, and it is not very difficult to imagine that he could have explained them orally to his disciples. ("The Thesis of Parmenides," in *Essays on Being* [New York: Oxford University Press, 2009], 150–151)

Kahn then detects a further ambiguity in the use of the veridical (nonexistential) employment of the verb *to be*—one that reflects a duality of veridical beings. Hence he writes:

> 'To be true' is not quite the same thing as 'to be the case.' What is true or false is normally a statement made in words [in other places he also talks of "intentional content" as that which is true or false]; what is the case or not the case is a fact or situation in the world.[6]

Kahn thereby takes the following supposition to be a natural one: an account of truth in terms of a correspondence between two sorts of veridical being is implicit in the veridical use of the verb *to be*.

Kahn construes the uses of *esti* in the positive and negative ways of Parmenides's poem as cases of the employment of the verb *to be* in its veridical sense. The strongest evidence he adduces for this reading is the poem's reference to truth / reality as the goal of inquiry.

While his highlighting of the veridical sense of the verb *to be* in Greek philosophy in general, and in Parmenides's poem in particular, is appropriate, I would argue that Kahn's separation of the intrinsic being of the veridical from its veridical being and his resulting association of the veridical sense with a corresponding account of truth are mistaken—both philosophically and exegetically.

There are all sorts of reasons one might hesitate to ascribe a correspondence theory of truth to the ancient Greek philosophers. But it suffices for our purposes simply to note that the goddess's statement that "thinking and being are the same" seems to leave no room for the notion of a correspondence between thinking and being.

Kahn himself, guided by his view of the veridical use of *to be*, unpacks Parmenides's account by invoking a distinction between a formal thesis and a semantical-ontological thesis:

> Parmenides offers a thesis not about the entailment relation between certain propositions but about the necessary connection between knowledge *(noein)* and its object, and his claim can be adequately expressed only in ontological terms. In the material mode, then, the thesis may be rendered as: "It (whatever

---

[6] Kahn, "The Greek Verb 'To Be,' and the Concept of Being," in *Essays on Being*, 25.

we can know, or whatever there is to be known) is a definite fact, an actual state of affairs."[7]

Kahn here imports a way of distinguishing between the formal and the material that is utterly alien to the Greek philosophers. Properly taking up the interpretative task of laying bare the degree of anachronism involved here would take us too far afield.[8] It is more important for present purposes to appreciate precisely how such a reading severs the relation between the Parmenidean challenge and the task of philosophical logic.

Put briefly, philosophical logic cannot attain the sort of mutual illumination to which it aspires unless it is able to reveal that there is no logical gap between the premise and the conclusion in each of the following two inferences—from 1 to 2 and from 1* to 2*:

1. He is pale.
2. We who think that he is pale are right. (We think what is true.)

1*. She is not pale.
2*. Those who think that she is pale are wrong. (They think what is false.)

---

[7] Kahn, "The Thesis of Parmenides," 154.

[8] What is imported in Greek philosophy here stems from a contemporary conception of logic as the metalinguistic study of formal languages (and the related idea that what the logician does is study ordinary language through the lens of formal languages). Such a conception cannot be regarded as a guise of philosophical logic in the sense indicated above, since it separates that which philosophical logic must clarify through a mutual illumination. That is, it breaks up the unified task of philosophical logic into two distinct tasks: that of adumbrating a formal characterization of the language and that of supplying a universe of possible semantic values for the expressions of that language. By contrast, it is worth noting that, unlike most contemporary analytic philosophy, Frege has not yet abandoned the presuppositionless task of philosophical logic. Frege's logical system is meant to be a universal language—one in which all reasoning is to be expressed in a manner that renders the inferential dependency of judgments on premises perspicuous and the character of logical truth fully apparent. Hence, in a fully adequate *Begriffsschrift*, no distinction can any longer be drawn between logical differences that are internal to thinking and categorical ones that are internal to the order of what is. In saying this, I am joining the ongoing scholarly debate over the question whether Frege's system requires or even so much as allows for a metatheoretical stance. I take it that Frege seeks to construct his *Begriffsschrift* in such a manner that, once we have fully entered it, there is neither any place, nor any need, for semantic talk. Hence, for him, in the actual conduct of serious human discursive activity—one in which truth is at stake—there is no

Correctly viewed, such inferences manifest the dependency of the truth or falsity of a judgment on what *is* or *is not* the case. In so doing, they resist Kahn's separation of the order of entailment from the order of relation to the object. Consequently, the distinction that Kahn here imports in order to clarify what is at stake in Parmenides's poem—one that insists upon such a separation—fails to appreciate how reflection on the challenge the poem presents may lead us to the very idea of philosophical logic.

2. The Two Ways

Just after the passage from the poem cited above, Parmenides declares: *"to gar auto noein estin te kai einai"*: "thinking and being are the same." This is fragment B3 of the poem.

A common assumption in the literature (held, for example, by Diels and Kranz) is that this fragment completes the last line of fragment B2, and should be read as a premise in the refutation of the negative way. If we read this assumption in the light of Kahn's interpretation of *esti,* we shall be led to conclude that what fragment B3 means to say is that thinking reaches all the way to that which is the case—that there is no gap between the thought that something is the case and something's being the case. This allows us to hear the goddess's argument against the negative way as taking the following form: Since it belongs to the very nature of *thinking* to reach all the way to that which is the case, negation and falsehood (which consist in the attempt to think that which is not the case) cannot be comprehended; negation and falsehood are therefore unintelligible.

I would like to propose that one misreads the claim of fragment B3 (that thinking and being are the same) if one thinks it leaves a place for an account of truth in terms of an idea of the correspondence of thinking with being. More generally, one misreads it if one thinks it leaves a place for *any*

---

place for notions such as "reference," "sense," truth as an "object," etc. The place of these notions in Frege's own writings is heuristic and transitional: they assist us in fully entering the sphere of serious human discursive activity. Hence, when viewed from the vantage point of fulfilling the aspiration of a properly philosophical logic, the internal flaw in Frege's logic lies in its inability to provide a genuine logical foothold, within the activity of serious thinking, for the notion of truth- and falsity-conditions for judgments and assertions.

account according to which the truth of thinking depends on something which is external to thinking.

It may appear as though we can secure the intelligibility of negation and falsehood by opening up a gap between thinking and being—abandoning the sameness of being and thinking in favor of a notion of thinking as a representation which is true or false in virtue of something in reality that is extrinsic to the activity of thinking, and to which thinking is related, or which thinking indicates. This may seem to be a small price to pay. But the claim that thinking and being are the same should be understood as an expression of a straightforward logical point. Peter Geach expresses the point in question as follows:

> For suppose A judges that Jupiter is round: call this judgment J1. If A reflects minimally, A will also be able to judge: My judgment that Jupiter is round is true; call this judgment J2. J1 and J2 clearly stand, and indeed both stand, together: they are not made true on two different accounts. Given that J2 is a first-person judgment simultaneous with J1, A who judges J1 needs no further justification, no additional data, to go on to J2. But on the theory of truth as correspondence to facts, J1's truth would be its correspondence to the roundness of Jupiter, and J2's truth would be its correspondence to a quite different fact, namely, J1's correspondence to the roundness of Jupiter. This is good enough reason to reject the theory; all the same . . . it taught us something: an adequate theory of truth must pass the test that this theory failed, namely, that J1 and J2 are made true in the same way and not on different accounts.[9]

What this shows is that there is no gap between one's judging something *(p)* and one's assessment of the same judgment as true ("I am truly judging *p*"). The transition from a judgment to a truth-assessment of that judgment is not based on a recognition of any new fact. A proper philosophical account of this matter must allow us to say that the assessment of one's judgment as true is internal to the very act of judging. The conception of thinking as the representation of a reality external to it does not allow us to say this. It opens up a logical gap between one's judgment and one's assessment of one's judgment as true, since it requires that the assessment concerns a relation between the thinking and something external to it.

---

[9] Peter Geach, "Truth and God," *Proceedings of the Aristotelian Society,* Supplementary Volume LVI (1982): 84.

The Parmenidean puzzle arises from the conjunction of the following two truisms: (i) the use of negation and the assessment of a statement as false are perfectly intelligible, and (ii) there is no logical gap between truly thinking that such-and-such is the case and such-and-such's being the case. But to affirm (i), we must refuse to follow the goddess's lead. For she tells us that negation and falsehood have no place in serious discourse that aims at the truth. Her point is that the truth of (ii) rules out the possibility of (i). The task of philosophical logic initially comes into view here as the task of accounting for the truth of (ii) in a manner that does not rule out the possibility of (i). In the end, we shall see that there is no way to do this as long as these appear to be two separate points—that is, in such a way that they appear to require being brought into some form of alignment with one another.

It might seem that the puzzlement can be easily removed—and a happy alignment between the two points achieved—by bringing particular Fregean notions to bear on the difficulty. Following Frege, we can say that the truth or falsity of a thought depends on something extrinsic to it—extrinsic to its logical identity as a thought. Yet the veridical verb "… is true" does not express any intrinsic or relational property of a thought. Now, the suggestion will be that the puzzle disappears once we recognize that when we talk of the facts of the world all we are talking about are true thoughts, in other words, that what is the case is simply a thought that is true.[10]

In order to see how this Fregean attempt to make our puzzlement vanish in fact fails to come to terms with the real difficulty, we shall need to appreciate how it turns on the assumption that being true or false originally involves a dissociation of what is true or false from the activity of thinking or saying that such-and-such is or is not the case; or in other words, on a dissociation of the intrinsic propositional unity of veridical being from its veridical being or non-being.[11] It will be essential to the project of this inquiry to show that this assumption is incoherent.

---

[10] For a proposal of this kind see John McDowell, *Mind and World* (Cambridge, MA: Harvard University Press, 1996), 26–27; and for a further development of this proposal, see Jennifer Hornsby, "Truth: The Identity Theory," *Proceedings of the Aristotelian Society* (1997): 1–24.

[11] This dissociation is the target of TLP 4.063, which purports to show that "the verb of a proposition is not 'is true' or 'is false' as Frege thought: rather that which 'is true' must already contain the verb" (Ludwig Wittgenstein, *Tractatus Logico-Philosophicus*, trans. Pears and McGuiness [Oxford: Blackwell, 2001], 29).

3. Syllogisms of Thinking and Being

Ludwig Wittgenstein returned again and again throughout his career to puzzles that arise from the use of the *veridical verb* in making seemingly straightforward points about the truth and falsehood of positive and negative judgments. Let us consider two such remarks by way of preparation for considering a third. The first concerns the falsehood of a simple positive judgment:

> How can one think what is not the case? If I think King's College is on fire when it is not on fire, the fact of its being on fire does not exist. Then how can I think it?[12]

The second concerns the truth of a simple negative judgment:

> It is the mystery of negation: This is not how things are, and yet we can say *how* things are *not*.[13]

Both of these puzzles are concerned with saying or thinking *something* that *is not*—that is therefore *nothing*.[14]

---

[12] L. Wittgenstein, *The Blue and Brown Books* (Oxford: Blackwell, 1969), 31.

[13] L. Wittgenstein, *Notebooks 1914–1916*, trans. Elizabeth Anscombe (Oxford: Blackwell, 1979), 30.

[14] Over the course of its history, analytic philosophy has associated different modes of non-existence with different components of a simple proposition. One of the early contributions of the tradition was the construal of non-existence claims as concerning the extensions of predicates through the use of quantifiers. Once issues of non-existence that could be understood in terms of empty extensions of predicates were set aside, the interest of analytic philosophers turned to the mode of non-existence associated with the singular term in a simple proposition, and hence to issues such as the status of vacuous names and fictional entities. While the problems of intentionality and non-existence, analytic philosophers remained notably untroubled by the problems under discussion here—ones that arise in connection with the proposition as a whole. The adoption of the force / content distinction allowed them to construe that which is true / false or is / is-not the case (e.g., a thought, a sentence, a state of affairs) as having its own existence independent of that conferred upon it through the veridical use of the verb "to be." Hence they were assured by the force / content distinction that the existence of the underlying propositional whole is guaranteed. Analytic philosophy thus became completely unconcerned with the problem of non-existence associated with the propositional

The aim of this book is to show that these puzzles pertain to the logical validity of certain inferences—forms of validity which are expressed in what I call the *syllogisms of thinking and being*.

Here are two examples of such syllogisms:

(1) A thinks p (1*) A thinks not-p
(2) not-p (p is not the case)   (2*) not-p (p is not the case)
(3) A falsely thinks p (3*) A truly thinks not-p

By a *syllogism* I mean here a sequence of propositions—premises and a conclusion—such that there is no logical gap between jointly holding the premises and holding the conclusion. Syllogism, in this sense, ultimately reflects which judgments are such that they can be held together in a single consciousness. This understanding of syllogism is to be contrasted with Frege's conception of inference as turning on what one is entitled to conclude given those judgments that one antecedently holds to be true. We shall have to examine Frege's conception carefully. This examination will lead us to the discovery that the overarching unity internal to any judgment is its compossibility with other judgments in a single consciousness.

The task of philosophical logic is to attain clarity concerning propositional signs in a way that will allow us to recognize—in a single glance—not only that all such syllogisms, when considered individually, are self-evidently true,

---

whole—hence with the difficulties raised by Parmenidean puzzles. The aim of this work is to show that the very notion of a forceless truth-bearer is an illusion through and through, and hence that the difficulties of non-existence associated with the propositional whole—precisely those which are at issue in those puzzles—are inescapable. (This does not mean that they cannot be overcome; but it does mean that they cannot be circumvented.) There is an historical irony in the fact that one of the uncontroversially original contributions of analytic philosophy—Russell's theory of descriptions—lay precisely in its having revealed that puzzles concerning naming and non-existence are mere illusions, arising from a confusion of names with predicates. If analytic philosophy had drawn the right lesson from Russell's theory, it would allow it to focus on the far deeper difficulties concerning non-existence associated with the propositional whole. In ignoring them, contemporary analytical philosophy ignores the fundamental problems of philosophical logic.

but that when considered together they are *substantially the same.*[15] This requires seeing that their self-evidence lies in their nondistinctness.

We recognize the logical unity of the assertions p and not-p by seeing p as a logical unit that recurs in the proposition not-p. But this leaves us with the following question: What is it for p to *occur* in another proposition? Certain common answers to this question erect insurmountable obstacles to the idea that the syllogisms of thinking and being are of a sort that can be recognized as self-evident.

For example, it is widely accepted, to the point that it is almost a dogma of contemporary philosophy, that we must acknowledge a radical difference between the occurrence of p in extensional truth-functional complexes (such as "~p") and its occurrence in intensional non-truth-functional complexes (such as "A thinks that p"). Given the way this distinction between logical contexts is usually understood, it has the consequence that, if one wants to answer our above question (what is it for p to occur in propositions of both of these sorts?), one must conclude that the p in question possesses the logically *prior* character of being something which is in and of itself true or false. "Prior" here means, first of all, prior to the logical unity of the pair of contradictory judgments p and not-p. This means that an account of the *internal logical complexity* of p is separable from an account of the logical unity of the contradictory pair. In other words, we can ask how the truth value of p is determined in isolation from the role it plays in the proposition not-p. Such a conception of the logical character of p debars us from being able to see as truistic any inference which involves a move from a context in which p occurs merely extensionally to one in which it is embedded in a statement about what a subject thinks or judges.

We noted above that contemporary philosophy insists upon a difference in what it is for one proposition to occur in another. That is, between

---

[15] By removing the obstacles that stand in the way of seeing that the syllogisms are self-evident, we shall also have removed the obstacles that stand in the way of seeing that, on the one hand, (1) and (1*) are logical contraries (in the sense that they cannot be held together) and, on the other hand, that p and not-p are a contradictory pair, such that not-p being the case is simply the same as p not being the case, and so on. Seeing things from this point of view, we shall be able to say that the logical and psychological principles of noncontradiction are neither different nor the same.

the way in which p occurs in an extensional truth-functional complex (such as "$\sim p$") and the way in which it occurs in an intensional non-truth-functional complex (such as "A thinks that p"). Underlying this distinction is a uniform conception of logical complexity—one according to which the manner in which a logical component occurs in a wider context is such that it must always be a *functional* component of that larger logical whole. It is a consequence of such a conception that it necessarily remains obscure how the syllogisms of thinking and being could ever qualify as truistically valid.

Donald Davidson's intervention into this tangle of difficulties is of interest here.[16] Davidson tries to reject the fashionable assumption of a radical difference in the character of the two sorts of logical contexts mentioned above by denying that p logically occurs at all (or is in any way contained) in "A judges p." We can see Davidson here as trying to close the formal gap created by the introduction of the idea that p occurs ambiguously across intensional and extensional contexts. But his manner of closing the gap comes at the price of having to deny that p ever occurs as a logical component in indirect speech. He deserves credit for seeing that something about the contemporary conception of what it is for one proposition to occur in another must be amiss, but he does not sufficiently press the question of what in this conception is inadequate. Hence he is unable to reveal the validity of the syllogisms of thinking and being and thus cannot account for our understanding of the notions of truth and falsity.[17]

4. The Uniqueness of Thinking

This brings us to our third remark from Wittgenstein. Here is *Philosophical Investigations,* §95:

---

[16] See Donald Davidson, "On Saying That," in *Inquiries Into Truth and Interpretation* (Oxford: Clarendon Press, 2001).

[17] Yet his program is based on the assumption that a speaker is capable of recognizing these syllogisms as valid. See Savas L. Tsohatzidis, "Truth Ascriptions, Falsity Ascriptions, and the Paratactic Analysis of Indirect Discourse," *Logique et Analyse* 232 (2015): 527–534.

"Thinking must be something unique." When we say, *mean,* that such-and-such is the case, then, with what we mean, we do not stop anywhere short of the fact, but mean: *such-and-such—is—so-and-so.*—But this paradox (which indeed has the form of a truism) can also be expressed in this way: one can *think* what is not the case.[18]

"Thinking must be something unique." This is a cry of astonishment. It is provoked by the sameness of thinking and being. The claim of sameness—and the correlative rejection of correspondence—is said to be a paradox expressed in the form of a truism. Then comes what we might have mistaken for a different paradox, one also expressed as a truism—one that, once it has been reformulated, is easily recognizable as encapsulating the Parmenidean puzzle of negation.

This compressed passage is out to reveal the identity of the philosophical problem that emerges in these apparently distinct guises. The two puzzles that figure in our earlier pair of remarks from Wittgenstein are also here brought together here and revealed to be part of a single puzzle. These in turn are revealed to be in no way distinct from the challenge of how to think the sameness of thinking and being—where what is at issue throughout the passage is what is expressed at its outset: that thinking must be something unique (*Einzigartiges*).

Here, *thinking,* in the first instance, means judging or asserting that such-and-such is the case, or that such-and-such is not the case. Once we have removed the misunderstandings that stand in the way of our being able to recognize—in a single glance—that the syllogisms of thinking and being are self-evident, then the uniqueness of thinking will become apparent. A major concern of this book is the different ways in which philosophers have failed to acknowledge—or even denied—the uniqueness of thinking in philosophy. Such failures to acknowledge the uniqueness of thinking—by conflating thinking with activities that are not thinking, or by conflating thinkers with beings that are not thinkers—render the validity of the syllogisms of thinking and being, and thus the notion of objectively valid judgment, unintelligible.

---

[18] L. Wittgenstein, *Philosophical Investigations,* trans. P. M. S Hacker and J. Schulte (Oxford: Blackwell, 2007).

I shall briefly indicate here two examples of these kinds of conflation, each of which will be discussed in more detail in the course of the book. First, *logical naturalism,* in both its ancient and modern guises, denies the uniqueness of thinking by placing the study of thinking within the study of natural activities. Second, *logical iconism,* which leads to the assimilation of thinking to perception, denies the uniqueness of thinking by construing thinking as a type of depiction or mirroring of reality. The logical unity of a judgment and its negation cannot be captured either in naturalistic or iconic terms.

The most elementary failure to acknowledge the uniqueness of thinking consists in the assimilation of thinking to naming or mentioning something.[19] In his *Sophist,* in the context of struggling with the Parmenidean puzzles, Plato introduces this crucial point that saying or asserting something is different from naming or mentioning. Thus he notes that the simplest judgment or assertion (i.e., *logos*) is true or false in virtue of being a combination of two types of expression—a name and a verb—each of which plays a different logical role. The name singles out the subject and the verb signifies something said about the subject—a determination of the subject.

Once this idea of a combination as the simplest site of truth and judgement is in place, the various ways of failing to acknowledge the uniqueness of thinking can be seen to turn on an assimilation of the complexity and unity of non-simple *logoi* to that of combinations.[20] Specifically, on an assimilation of simple judgments to predicative determination[21] (this is not, I shall argue, a mistake that Plato himself makes). This uniform conception of the logical complexity of thinking involves the isolation of a combination—the simplest *logos*—as a semantically autonomous unit from *logoi* which are not simple. We shall find that when all thinking is construed as predicative determination, then even predicative unity itself—and hence

---

[19] Recall, for example, the argument, presented by a sophist in the *Euthydemus,* that is based on an assimilation of thinking to mentioning something. That argument purports to show that the very idea of genuine disagreement between speakers is unintelligible. See *Euthydemus* 285d7–286d4.

[20] A symptom of this failure is the view of the proposition or a sentence as a shadow of a fact (cf. *Philosophical Investigations* §94).

[21] "*S* is not *F*" can be assimilated to "*S* is *F*" in two ways. Firstly, one can treat "not *F*" as another determination word; on this account, positive and negative predication differ merely in predicative content. Secondly, one can treat *is-not* as a different copula; on this account, positive and negative predication differ merely in predicative form.

the difference between naming and saying (or between the name and the verb) on which Plato insists in the *Sophist*—cannot be comprehended.

In order to see the syllogisms of thinking and being as self-evident, we shall need to comprehend the embedding of one propositional sign in another in nonpredicative (indeed, in nonfunctional) terms. If what we said earlier is true, namely, that an assertion such as "*S* is *F*" cannot be comprehended separately from its contradictory pairing with "*S* is not-*F*,"[22] then an understanding of simple predicative unity will require a comprehension of the nonpredicative character of the manner in which propositional signs are embedded in one another.

If the foregoing is right, then the contradictory difference between "*S* is *F*" and "*S* is not-*F*" cannot be a predicative difference in content or form;[23] similarly, "*A* thinks *p*" can be a predicative determination neither of a thinker nor of the proposition thought. Therefore, that which is expressed by something of the form "*S* thinks that *p*" should not be logically assimilated to that which is expressed by sentences such as "*S* is doing ϕ" or "*S* is ϕ-ing" (which nevertheless have a superficially similar form). The "thinks" in "*S* thinks" is an activity in what is logically a fundamentally different sense of "activity" from any expressed by verbs in predicative propositions of the form "*S* is ϕ-ing."[24] In coming to appreciate this difference between thinking and acting, we are able to detect the logical uniqueness of thinking. We misunderstand this uniqueness if we construe it in terms of the exceptional nature

---

[22] This requirement should not be confused with Frege's context principle, according to which we can only ask for the meaning of an expression in the context of a proposition. Frege's requirement is limited to the context of atomic propositions whereas this requirement applies to other propositional contexts, and can thus be described as the full context principle.

[23] As we shall see later, if the assumption that all logical complexity is predicative or functional in nature remains in place, then the difference between a pair of contradictory claims—between (a) "*S* is *F*" and (b) "*S* is not-*F*"—must be construed as either predicative or functional in nature. There are two available options for making sense of such a construal: one either traces the difference to (1) two ways of predicating one and the same predicate of the subject, or to (2) predicating two different predicates of the subject. Each leads to a dead end: (1) obliterates the logical unity of (a) and (b); (2) implies that what is true or false about an individual—its being *F*—is independent of the contradictory unity of the pair of predications "*S* is *F*" and "*S* is not-*F*."

[24] Both my usage and my understanding of the Aristotelian terminology of capacity and activity are informed by Jonathan Beere's illuminating study, *Doing and Being* (Oxford: Oxford University Press, 2009).

of either the substances or the attributes involved in a nexus of predication. The uniqueness we seek to understand here has nothing to do with the specialness of some particular sort of predicative content.

To capture these points we shall introduce the terminology of *categorematic* and *syncategorematic* expressions. A categorematic expression can be a component of a predicative proposition, whereas a syncategorematic expression cannot be a component of a predicative proposition. The basic syncategorematic expressions are predicative propositions themselves; but there are further syncategorematic expressions that have the outward grammatical form of incomplete expressions—such as "*A* thinks __" in our above example—that require completion by a propositional sign. As we shall see, syncategorematic differences between propositions or judgments, in contrast to categorematic differences, do not correspond to any bit of reality.

Reflection upon this point will lead us, in what follows, to conclude that the difference between "*p*" and "I think *p*" (and hence the difference between consciousness and self-consciousness) is syncategorematic—and so too is the difference between *p* and not-*p*. This difference lies in the employment of syncategorematic expressions and cannot be associated with a difference in predicative content or form. The consciousness of one's thinking must involve the identification of its syncategorematic difference, and hence is essentially tied up with the use of language.

In the end, we shall see that the various capacities which philosophical logic finds itself called upon to elucidate—capacities for judgment, for language, for the deployment of logical words (such as "not" and "and"), and for self-consciousness (and hence for the use of the word "I")—are all one and the same capacity. To appreciate this is to appreciate the uniqueness of thinking. And to fully appreciate this is to come to see that here even the concept of a *capacity* threatens to block our way to a full appreciation of the uniqueness of thinking.

A further complication that will emerge relatively late in our inquiry is the manner in which some expressions—such as "I" and the proper names of human beings—can occur in both syncategorematic and categorematic contexts. A human thinker is also a determinable being. This book presents us with the task of trying to understand our being, the being of human beings, as that of determinable thinkers.

5. The Unity of the Logically Two-Way

Alexander Mourelatos has proposed a reading of Parmenides's *Poem* that breaks with the standard interpretation by denying that *esti* is a complete copula. Mourelatos holds that in the goddess's description of the two ways, *esti* and *ouk esti* indicate a pair of propositional frames—"__ is __" and "__ is not __"—with unspecified subjects and predicates. As such, he argues that they should be construed as displaying positive and negative predication, respectively.

Mourelatos also rejects the entire form of account that characterizes standard interpretations of *how* the goddess purports to show that any use of negation is unintelligible. All such accounts understand the goddess as arguing that negation presupposes the nonexistence of something. On Mourelatos's alternative reading, the goddess instead purports to show that negation must be unintelligible by arguing that a negated predicate must be meaningless or nonsensical.

He illustrates his reading of the refutation of the negative way with a Homeric figure:

> [T]he logic of Parmenides' argument is intimately tied with the central heuristic image of a cognitive journey to the *eon*, "what is" or *aletheia,* "reality." For if I should start the journey to *F,* say to the island of Ithaca, there is a course I can follow and I can ultimately complete my journey and reach my destination; if I should start on a journey to not *F,* not to the island of Ithaca, I wander endlessly. (A. Mourelatos, "Some Alternatives in Interpreting Parmenides," *The Monist* 62:1 [1979]: 10)

According to his reading, the goddess makes the point that the negation of a predicate (e.g., *not-beautiful*) does not signify a possible determination of something. She concludes from this that the negation of a predicate does not say anything about the subject and therefore must be meaningless. This forms the basis, according to Mourelatos's reading, of the case she brings against the negative way.[25]

---

[25] In what follows, we shall see that the attempt to resist this conclusion via a semantic analysis of negative predicates in terms of a disjunction of predicates (or some other form of relation) that are incompatible with positive predicates must fail.

Of course, our use of negated predicates is perfectly sound; this is precisely what gives rise to the puzzle. Mourelatos takes it that this puzzle is different from that which arises in connection with the veridical sense of "to be"—the one that is at issue in the passages from Wittgenstein quoted above.

We saw that on Charles Kahn's understanding of the latter sort of puzzle, the intrinsic being of propositionally structured items is to be understood as independent of their being true or being false. (Similarly, Frege takes the being of thought to be independent of its being true or being false.) Indeed, as long as the being conferred by the veridical copula is thus taken to be external to the propositional unity of the veridical being, the puzzle Mourelatos takes to form the basis of the goddess's case and the one that concerns Wittgenstein must necessarily appear to be distinct puzzles.

Pace Kahn, the veridical uses of "to be" and "not to be" are not external to simple propositional unity. They cannot be applied to this form of unity from without. If the veridical uses of these expressions do not take independently unified propositional complexes as their subjects, then they must somehow pertain to that which does not simply lie outside of such complexes. This leaves us with the task of showing how the difference between the veridical uses of "to be" and of "not to be" are instead associated with differences located in the verbs (i.e., in the predicates) that occur within simple propositions and the negation of those verbs, respectively.

Once we come to appreciate the nonexternality of the veridical to predicative unity, we are able to recognize that the puzzle concerning the veridical use of "not to be" and the puzzle concerning the meaningfulness of negative predication are but two guises of one and the same difficulty.

Recall what we said above, that the challenge here is to achieve a point of view on these matters from which, in a single logical glance, the syllogisms of thinking and being can all be recognized as self-evident. Those syllogisms were schematically given above as having p as their overt common logical element—occurring in contexts specified as "p," "not-p," "I think p," etc. The upshot of the association of the veridical and predicative is that the attainment of this aim requires that we turn our attention to instances of these syllogisms in which "S is F" is substituted for "p" and "S is not-F" is substituted for "not-p."

Aristotle offers a helpful pointer toward the path we must follow if we are to attain this aim. This pointer, however, can easily lead to mistaking the correct path for one that leads to a dead end. He identifies the members of a contradictory pair of simple predications as consisting in a *combination (synthesis)* and a *separation (diairhesis)* respectively. He thereby provides us with a way of redescribing our problem: What does it mean to understand the difference between the members of a contradictory pair in terms of combination and separation?

Let us first consider the dead end. One may hear Aristotle as proposing here that we construe "*S* is *F*" and "*S* is not-*F*" as involving a pair of contrasting relations between what is signified by the subject-term of the judgment and what is signified by its predicate. It will be shown that, if we allow such a construal, that which logically unites negative and positive predication is lost.

How do we avoid this dead end? The puzzle of the meaningfulness of a negated predicate (which, as we have indicated above, is not distinct from the puzzle of veridical being) will disappear once we recognize that the difference between the predicate and the negation of the predicate is only syncategorematic—or, to put the same point differently: that the contradictory difference between combination and separation is not a predicative difference. How are we to understand this nonpredicative difference between positive and negative predication?

Mourelatos criticizes conventional interpretations of Parmenides for ignoring the imagery and *topoi* of the journey: the alternate route, the boundary, *the way*—which he takes as providing models for the main doctrines of the *Poem*. Employing an expression that has its place within this field of *topoi*, I shall make use of the notion of a *two-way capacity*—which Aristotle introduces in *Metaphysics* Theta 2—in order to elucidate the internal syncategorematic unity of a contradictory pair.[26]

We shall see later on in this book that there is a deep difference between the general kind of rational capacity that is Aristotle's topic in Theta 2 and the kind that is our concern here. I use (and thus appropriate for my own purposes) Aristotle's term "two-way capacity" specifically for those *logical* two-way capacities for judgment that I am about to discuss. Two-wayness is, for Aristotle, the mark of a rational capacity (for change). Rational capacities for Aristotle are associated with the verb (healing or poisoning), with

---

[26] My employment of the useful qualifier "two-way" is indebted to Stephen Makin's introduction to and commentary on his translation of *Metaphysics Book Theta* (Oxford: Oxford University Press, 2006).

something inside the proposition; logical capacities are associated with the whole proposition ("*S* is *F*"). That I am able to appropriate his term for my own purposes in this way shows that these two cases share something in common while nevertheless remaining logically different—a difference I mark by calling the former categorematic capacities and the latter syncategorematic (or logical) capacities.

I wish to propose that the contradictory judgments "*S* is *F*" and "*S* is not-*F*" are to be understood as the positive and negative acts of a single two-way logical capacity—which, as we shall see, can be specified through its positive act: "*S* is *F*." The capacity is *asymmetrical,* since the positive act is prior to the negative. This means that the only predicative determination in a simple contradictory pair is the *positive* predication. Yet even the positive case is essentially one of a *pair* of acts.

Negative predication brings the positive determination of the other member of the contradictory pair into play. But it does so through what I shall call a *display* of the positive act of predication. Through this display, what the negative act specifically represents is that nothing of the positive determination pertains to the subject, hence the priority of the positive over the negative act. Between the positive and the negative acts of predication there is only ever a single determination in play. Therefore, the difference between the two cases is not a predicative difference. Rather, it is an example of what I shall call a *syncategorematic difference.*

This notion of an asymmetric logical (or syncategorematic) two-way capacity will allow us to construe the truth and falsity of affirmation and negation in terms of the sameness and difference of the manner in which a single logical capacity is active in a judgment and a state of affairs. This logical notion of a two-way capacity provides us with a way of understanding what is at stake in Aristotle's terminology of combination and separation: combination and separation are the positive and negative acts of a single logical two-way capacity. The capacity is one *for* combination; the negative act, the separation, is based on a display of the combination. We might put this by saying it is *a separation from the combination.*

Following J. S. Mill, we distinguished at the outset between a *complete* (or absolute or one-place) use of "is" (which is not complemented by a predicate) and an *incomplete* (or predicative or two-place) use of "is." What our discussion has just shown is that the latter—predicative unity—can be seen in two ways. We thus require a further crucial distinction between these two senses of two-place or predicative being. In fact, such a distinction is implicit in the account offered above of the syncategorematic unity of the contradictory pair.

These two senses correspond to the double-sidedness—and hence to two ways of looking at—the verb of a simple predicative proposition. The verb can be associated with the positive predication, on the one hand, or with the syncategorematic unity of the contradictory pair, on the other. Considered solely in its first guise, the verb signifies a determination of the subject—something that can be truly asserted of it. Considered from within the unity of the contradictory pair, the verb is associated with a two-way capacity. This double-sidedness is completely destroyed if one fails to appreciate (1) the priority of positive to negative predication and, *at one and the same time,* (2) the dominance of the unity of the contradictory pair over each of its members.[27]

The double-sidedness of the simple positive predicative proposition can be seen through the corresponding double-sidedness of its verb. Regarded from one direction, restricting our view to what happens *within* the positive proposition, it signifies a state or determination of the subject;[28] regarded from the other, widening our view so as to include the entirety of the contradictory pair of which it is a member, the verb governs *the unity of the whole* that can be negated.

The verb understood in accordance with the first of these two senses is to be associated with a reality that inheres in the positive *fact.* For example, both Venus and Helen *are* beautiful; Quasimodo is not. Venus and Helen have beauty in common with one another, but not with Quasimodo. We can therefore speak of the attribute ("beauty") commonly exemplified by Venus and Helen, or the concept under which they both fall, or the form in which they jointly participate—and which Quasimodo does not exemplify, fall under, or participate in. These logico-philosophical terms of art—"exemplifying" an "attribute," "falling under" a "concept," "participating in" a "form"—are all ways of glossing that two-place or predicative determination which is *internal* to

---

[27] It is tempting to describe (1) and (2) as the basic hermeneutical circle which is internal to simple assertions / propositions.

[28] Moreover, as we shall see in Chapter 2, from that direction we can come to see the verb as a determination of names in a proposition that exemplifies a formally similar determination of name bearers.

positive predicative facts. Anything which is logically internal to a positive predicative fact is—in my terminology—*categorematic.*

The second predicative or two-place sense is the veridical or copulative sense. The verb understood in a veridical sense displays a judgment or assertion, namely, an act of a two-way logical capacity or form. The judgments "Helen is beautiful" and "Quasimodo is not beautiful" are positive and negative acts of the syncategorematic (or logical) form "___ is beautiful."

These two acts go together with the veridical senses of "to be" and "not to be." Hence what is said above about the form of the capacity for judgment can also be said about the form of facts—for there is only one syncategorematic (or logical) form at issue throughout. Hence, we can equally say: the positive fact that Venus is beautiful and the negative fact that Quasimodo is not beautiful are different acts of this same logical form—i.e., combination and separation.

The reality of beauty as a determination is internal to the positive fact. The priority of the positive predication within a given contradictory pair means that all such predicative reality is in the positive facts. The priority of the positive case notwithstanding, even it (that such and such *is* the case) can be stated only through that which has the unity of judgment—through that which can be negated. From this, as the ensuing work will seek to show, one may conclude that the dominant sense of being is that of the veridical "to be" and "not to be."

6. The Hidden Thread

We now return to the gate of philosophy—to the choice between the two ways of inquiry. After rejecting the negative way, the goddess goes on to argue that coming-to-be (*genesis*) is impossible, so that being—the object of the investigation—must be without generation: imperishable, continuous, and unchangeable. Her reasoning rigorously sets forth, without the slightest compromise, a picture of all and only that which reality can contain if viewed from a perspective that is limited to the categorematic—that is, from one that takes the categorematic to be self-standingly intelligible.[29]

---

[29] From this perspective Geach's observation that there is no logical gap between my judgment and my assessment of my judgment as true appears to imply Parmenidean monism.

This refusal to compromise is a testimony to the rigor of Parmenides's thinking—its refusal to delude itself into imagining that negation can be captured in categorematic terms. Its insistence on the sameness of thinking and being is tied to its appreciation that thinking cannot be dependent for its success on anything that is external to it.

The young man standing at the gate of philosophy is stuck there. He cannot move: the negative way is impossible, while the positive way denies the very intelligibility of the was and will be of change and motion. The possibility of liberation from the framework of the gate—and its *forced choice of two ways*—is to be found in the unity of that which is *two-way* in the sense explicated above: namely, in the notion of thinking and being as the activity of a two-way syncategorematic or logical capacity.

This brings us back to the topic with which we began: the possibility of philosophical logic. This book seeks to articulate a conception that lives up to the original philosophical understanding of the task of logic. It shows that the success of such an enterprise requires the notion of a two-way syncategorematic or logical capacity outlined above. The ensuing account of philosophical logic purports to illuminate the categorical form of reality through an acknowledgment of the dominance of the syncategorematic. At one and the same time, in unfolding such an account, we seek to show that the idea of philosophical logic, so understood, constitutes a hidden thread that runs throughout the history of philosophy, from its originators in Plato and Aristotle to its most recent representative in Wittgenstein.

CHAPTER ONE

The Life of p

1. Principles of Noncontradiction

1.1.

To be a philosopher, according to Aristotle, is to be an authority on this principle:

> (OPNC) For the same thing to hold good and not to hold good simultaneously of the same thing and in the same respect is impossible (given any further specification which might be added against the dialectical difficulties). (Gamma 3, 1005b18–21)[1]

The authority comes from the extraordinary generality of philosophical understanding:

> It is appropriate for him who has the best understanding about each genus to be able to state the firmest principles of that actual subject, and hence, when his subject is *being qua being,* to state the firmest principles of everything: and this man is the philosopher. (Gamma 3, 1005b8–12)

---

[1]Quotations from Aristotle are drawn from the following translations: *Categories and De Interpretatione,* trans. J. L. Ackrill (Oxford: Oxford University Press, 1975); *Metaphysics Book B and K 1-2,* trans. A. Madigan (Oxford: Oxford University Press, 1999); *Metaphysics Book Gamma, Delta and Epsilon,* trans. C. Kirwan (Oxford: Oxford University Press, 1993); and *Metaphysics Book Theta,* trans. S. Makin (Oxford: Oxford University Press, 2006).

(Strictly speaking, there is only an analogy between a philosopher and a scientist; Aristotle says elsewhere that philosophy is not directed at any genus whatsoever.)

The remark about the philosopher should be read in the context of the second *aporia* of *Metaphysics* Beta, which Aristotle revisits in the opening of Gamma 3:

> We have to say whether it falls to one, or a different, science to deal with the things that in mathematics are termed axioms, and with substance.[2] (Gamma 3, 1005a19–21)

In Beta he called an axiom a "principle of reasoning." Such principles are

> the common opinions from which all people draw proofs—for example, that it is necessary either to affirm or to deny everything, and that it is impossible to be and not to be at the same time, and any other such propositions. (Beta 2, 996b26–30)

The *aporia* is finally resolved in Gamma, with its new characterization of first philosophy as the science of *being qua being*.[3] For now the principles of reasoning can be described as "holding of *being qua being*," and so:

> It is indeed obvious that the investigation of these [the axioms] too falls to one science, and that the philosopher's; for they hold good of being qua being and not of a certain genus, separate and distinct from others. (Gamma 3, 1005a21–24)

Because the axioms hold of being *qua* being, they are in play wherever truth is at stake—for example in the special sciences. But because of their

---

[2] The second *aporia* consists of considerations for and against the following thesis: There is one science that is: (1) the study of the different principles of reasoning, (2) the study of substance in general, (3) wisdom, the highest kind of knowledge.

[3] "[T]o people who confess that they are puzzled by the cryptic phrase 'to study being *qua* being,'" Crubellier says that

> one may give this clue: to consider beings *qua* being is to consider them from the point of view in which, for instance, the principle of non-contradiction tells us something about them. (Michel Crubellier, "Aporia 1-2," in Crubellier and Laks, eds., *Aristotle's Metaphysics Beta: Symposium Aristotelicum* [Oxford: Oxford University Press, 2009], 71)

peculiar generality they cannot be comprehended by studying a specific *kind* of beings. They cannot be incorporated within the subject matter of a special science.

Aristotle notes that while scientists such as geometers and arithmeticians must *use* these principles, they do not actually *investigate* them. The exceptions are certain students of nature, who mistakenly think that they can comprehend the principles as part of their field:

> But that is not surprising, since they alone have considered that they were investigating the whole of nature, i.e., that which is. But since there is someone still further above the student of nature (for nature is one particular genus of what there is), the investigation of these things must fall to him who studies what is universal and primary substance. The study of nature is also a wisdom but not primary. (Gamma 3, 100a32–35)

Their mistake is to identify nature with the whole of being. Nature *is* a whole, Aristotle says—but a *limited* one, since "there is someone still further above the student of nature": the philosopher. It is the philosopher who studies "what is universal and primary substance."

But what does this have to do with the other point—that it is the philosopher and not the natural scientist who studies the principles of reasoning?

The answer begins with a recognition that the object of natural science—the whole of nature—does not contain thinkers or thinking. The study of the intellect goes *beyond* physics. But that is only a beginning. We must explain this "beyond," and why the study of thinkers and thinking is more inclusive than the study of nature.

My suggestion will be that principles of reasoning apply to intellects as *principles of thinking*, but to natural substances and their predicative determinations as *principles of being*. In particular, nature can be identified with everything to which the law of noncontradiction applies merely as a principle of being, and so with all the predicative facts (both positive and negative.) It will turn out that the larger whole which includes thinking is not richer *in predicative content* than nature. In other words, nature includes every determinable and every determination. A study that goes beyond nature goes beyond these too.[4]

---

[4] The principle of noncontradiction applies to beings like us *both* as a principle of being *and* as a principle of thinking. We are thinkers, yes, but we are *also* determinables.

Natural scientists do not study the principles of reasoning as such. They do not reflect on them as principles of thinking, or on the unity of thinking and being.[5]

1.2.

Aristotle says that OPNC is the firmest principle because

(PPNC) It is impossible for anyone to believe that the same thing is and is not. (Gamma 3, 1005b22–25)

If OPNC is the *ontological principle of noncontradiction,* PPNC is the *psychological principle of noncontradiction.*[6] The ontological principle is a principle

---

A purely intellectual substance, a god, is not a subject of any predicative determination. For now, though, I will ignore such complications.

[5] According to Aristotle, a special science deals with the concepts and the generalizations that apply to beings insofar as they belong to "the subject genus of that science." We might think that the subject genus of the science of *being qua being* is simply *being,* so that first philosophy will be the science that deals with the concepts and principles that apply to beings simply insofar as they fall under the genus *being.* But—as I mentioned— Aristotle does not think that being is a genus. Why then does he speak of the *science* of being *qua* being?

In Gamma 2 Aristotle addresses this question by invoking *substances* as the primary *beings,* on which all the others depend for their being and intelligibility. Commentators sometimes conclude that substance is the subject genus of philosophy, so that philosophy is the science of substance. But this assumes that substance is itself a genus. It is not, for there is no single essence that natural and thinking substances share. (In fact they are radically different.) That is the point of Aristotle's remark in Gamma 3 that nature is a whole, but not the whole of being.

We shall see this more clearly as we consider the principle of noncontradiction. Generic differences between natural substances—for instance, the difference between plants and animals—will turn out to be *categorematic* differences, differences in modes of predication. (For an exposition of this kind of difference, see Matthew Boyle's "Essentially Rational Animals," in G. Abel and J. Conant, eds., *Rethinking Epistemology* [Berlin: De Gruyter, 2012].) But the difference between human beings, which are thinkers, and natural substances cannot be understood that way. It is a *syncategorematic* or a nonpredicative difference, corresponding to the difference between the principles of thinking and being. We can only understand the unity and division of substance in general in terms of *that* difference.

[6] In his influential monograph on the principle of noncontradiction, Łukasiewicz distinguishes between three formulations of the principles in Aristotle's work:

of being. It appears to place a limit on what can be. The psychological principle is a principle of thinking. It appears to place a limit on what can be believed or thought.[7]

Under the influence of *fin de siècle* anti-psychologism, commentators have become highly sensitive to possible confusions of OPNC and PPNC. But Aristotle often seems uninterested in the difference between them. Indeed, he calls OPNC a principle of reasoning.

1.3.

In Gamma 3, Aristotle derives PPNC directly from OPNC.

This is usually explained as follows. Suppose a believer is a sort of substance. And suppose a particular belief is a property of this substance. Having the belief that *p* is correlated with having the property expressed by the predicate Belief (. . . , *p*); not having this belief is correlated with the property expressed by the predicate not-Belief (. . . , *p*).[8] By OPNC, these predicates cannot be co-instantiated. PPNC follows.

Aristotle formulates the Law of Contradiction in three ways, as an ontological, a logical, and a psychological law; he does not make explicit the differences between them.

(a) Ontological formulation: "It is impossible that the same thing should both belong and not belong to the same thing at the same time and in the same respect." (Meta. IV 3, 1005b19–20)

(b) Logical formulation: "The most certain of all [principles] is that contradictory sentences are not true at the same time." (Meta. IV 6, 1011b13–14)

(c) Psychological formulation: "No-one can believe that the same thing can [at the same time] be and not be." (Meta. IV 3, 1005b23–24) ("Aristotle on the Law of Contradiction," in Barnes, Schofield and Sorabji, eds., *Articles on Aristotle Vol.3: Metaphysics* [New York: St. Martin's Press, 1979], 50–51)

The unity of (a) and (c) is a major theme of this chapter. The unity of (a) and (b)—and thus of all three formulations—is a major theme of Chapter 3.

[7] The figure of the limit here is misleading; we shall come to recognize that there is no limit to thoughts, "for in order to be able to draw a limit to thought, we should have to find both sides of the limit thinkable (i.e., we should have to be able to think what cannot be thought)" (Wittgenstein, *Tractatus Logico-Philosophicus*, 3). Moreover, there is no limit to the expression of thoughts since no expression can be rejected as transgressive, i.e., as lying outside the limit. This point is correctly emphasized by 'resolute' readers of Wittgenstein.

[8] Łukasiewicz notes that this proof is inadequate because "Aristotle did not demonstrate that beliefs answering to contradictory sentences are contraries." For "A believes *p*" can be false in two ways:

I am going to argue that all this is wrong—both in itself and as a reading of Aristotle. A believer is not a natural substance; a belief is not a property; nor are beliefs joined together in a believer as properties are joined together in a substance.[9] PPNC is not an instance of OPNC.

2. The Psycho-logical Problem

2.1.

It is often said that logical principles govern thinking. But what sort of government is this? And what is the source of its authority?

The philosophical concern that I try to convey by these questions can be described as *the psycho-logical problem*. We can distinguish four approaches to this problem corresponding to four views on the provenance of logical principles:

(1) Psycho-logicism: ←
(2) Logo-psychism: →
(3) Psycho / logical dualism: ≠
(4) Psycho / logical monism.[10]

These four approaches can be distinguished by their respective treatment of the difference between PPNC and OPNC.

  (i) A judges that not-*p*.
  (ii) A has no view on whether *p*.

Consequently, he says, not-Belief (. . . , *p*) cannot be identified with Belief (. . . , not-*p*). He is right, of course. But in my view the mistake lies not with Aristotle but with the interpretation.

[9] Later this will be revealed as the main insight of Kant's critical turn.

[10] There is a radical break between the first three approaches and the fourth that is obscured by the terminology. According to the first three approaches, the thinker is a substance and his thoughts are his intrinsic or relational states, but the fourth approach denies that thinking is a determination of a substance. The monism in question is therefore not a substance monism.

Psycho-logicism takes PPNC to be a law of our psychology, and OPNC as a report on how things look to us *given* PPNC. Logo-psychism takes PPNC to be an application of OPNC to human psychology. Whether the principle of noncontradiction is properly a principle of thinking or of being is a matter of serious disagreement between these different approaches. Nonetheless, they both agree on this: that there is in the end only *one* such principle.

Psycho / logical dualism takes PPNC and OPNC to be logically independent generalizations and denies that PPNC is a logical principle. To these, the dualist adds a *third* principle of noncontradiction, which is not a generalization but a normative requirement: that one *should* not contradict oneself.

Psycho / logical monism takes a belief or judgment to be a unity that is immanent and thus only identifiable within a larger unity—that of consciousness and language. Since a unity *in* consciousness is the same as a consciousness *of* unity, the monist holds that a belief or a judgment is as such self-conscious, and we shall come to see that such self-consciousness is essentially contained in the use of language. That is, we shall come to see that this self-consciousness is essentially the expression of consciousness by language. From the monist point of view, a simple propositional sign displays a possible act of consciousness, but the identity of this act depends on the uses of a proposition within other propositional contexts. Hence, for example, understanding p as an expression of consciousness depends on understanding the use of p in negation. As such, from this point of view we come to see that no conscious act is displayed or specified by the proposition of the form $(p$ and $\sim p)$ and therefore no judgment or assertion is displayed by $\sim(p$ and $\sim p)$. This means that $\sim(p$ and $\sim p)$ and $(p$ and $\sim p)$ are not genuine propositions. Understanding OPNC consists in seeing that the repetition of p in these logical contexts is self-cancelling. The difference between OPNC and PPNC will then correspond to the difference between the consciousness expressed by "p" and the self-consciousness expressed by "I think p." But this talk of "difference" does not mean that PPNC and OPNC are two different principles. In the end the monist will say *neither* that they are two, *nor* one. Or rather: that they are the same *and* different.

This is what I myself want to say.

2.2.

Frege singles out psycho-logicism[11] as the main obstacle to understanding the idea of thinking as governed by logic. He seems to have in mind a kind of logical naturalism—similar to the view that Aristotle criticizes in Gamma 3, which assigns the study of principles of reasoning to natural science.[12] If that were right, Frege says, such principles

> could be nothing but laws of psychology. . . . And if logic were concerned with these psychological laws it would be a part of psychology; it is in fact viewed in just that way. (*The Basic Laws of Arithmetic*, trans. Montgomery Furth [Berkeley: University of California Press, 1964], 12–13)

But (he says) this view is self-refuting. For it cannot ground the *normativity* of the logical requirements that underlie the objective purport of every claim about how things are—including the claims of psycho-logicism itself.[13] Frege's criticism of psycho-logicism is meant to bring out that the normative import of a judgment/belief lies in the judgeable content, and therefore that an episode of thinking is revealed as subject to logical assessments only by being associated with such content.[14]

[11] In contemporary philosophy the term *psychologism* denotes those programs which try to describe and explain human activity as a part of the order described and explained by the empirical sciences. (It is also used as a slur against ostensibly nonpsychologistic programs.) It is possible to be "psychologistic" with respect to some parts of the mind but not others. For example, Frege is psychologistic with respect to phenomenal episodes including sensations and images, but not with respect to thinking. But this division of the mind into logical and subjective parts is itself characteristic of psycho-logical dualism.

[12] There is a basic difference between the *nature* of modern science and the *physis* of the Aristotelians. Crudely, the Aristotelian scientist studies *natures* or forms, while the modern scientist studies a nature devoid of such forms. But in my view both types of naturalism make the same mistake: they assimilate all judgments to predicative determinations and thus in particular they treat "A thinks *p*" as a predicative *determination* of A.

[13] Both monism and dualism are opposed to psycho-logicism—but for different reasons. The dualist opposes psycho-logicism because it is *false*. (Frege's view is that the normative import of a belief or judgment lies in a logical identity that cannot be captured from a psycho-logical point of view.) The monist rejects psycho-logicism as *nonsensical*, and thus as providing only the illusion of an account.

[14] Here the Fregean recognizes the logical difference between humans and other beings: the descriptions of natural beings which are employed in the natural sciences gener-

Łukasiewicz accuses Aristotle of a fallacy in his understanding of the log-ical character of thinking which is the inverse of psycho-logicism:

> In the psychological investigation of acts of believing (*De Inter.,* c. 14) Aris-totle commits the very common fallacy of "logicism in psychology," which can pass as a counterpart for "psychologism in logic." Instead of investigating psychical functions, the Stagirite considers the propositions corresponding to them and their logical relations. ("Aristotle on the Law of Contradiction," in Barnes, Schofield, and Sorabji, eds., *Articles on Aristotle Vol.3: Meta-physics* [New York: St. Martin's Press, 1979])

The fallacy which can be called *logo-psychism* consists in assimilating be-liefs or judgments to contents, which are supposed to be independent of the mind—so that mere mental acts turn out to be logically related. But the main evidence Łukasiewicz cites for ascribing this view to Aristotle—the argu-ment for PPNC—assumes the veracity of what I called the "usual reading" of Gamma 3. And I do not think that is an innocent assumption.

Łukasiewicz's reading of Aristotle is based on the Fregean assimilation of anti-psycho-logicism to psycho-logical dualism. From this point of view, Aristotle's talk of acts of thinking as logically and semantically evaluable renders him guilty of assimilating acts to contents. In any case, I will argue that anti-psycho-logicism need not take the shape of psycho/logical dualism.

2.3.

The dualist approach to the psycho-logical problem is based on a theory of judgment as involving a subjective act and a truth-evaluable content—the unity and complexity of which is external to the judging subject. In other words, it is based on psycho/logical dualism.

The aim of such an approach is to escape the fallacy of psycho-logicism, which ignores the objectivity of propositional content, without falling into the fallacy of logo-psychism, which ignores the subjective act. Some version of this approach can be found in the Stoics' distinction between a judgment

---

ally—in contrast to those employed in the special science of psychology—do not men-tion content and are therefore extensional.

and a judgeable content *(lekta),* and in Descartes's account of judgment as a combination of will and understanding.[15]

But its most systematic advocate is Frege, who sought to design a logical symbolism *(Begriffsschrift)* that would show the logical identity of contents through the composition of propositional signs. In other words, it is a *functionalist* conception of logical complexity, and thus a *universalist* and *extensionalist conception* of logic.[16]

Frege's main conviction is that if the validity of an inference from a generalization to its instance is understood in terms of quantified propositions, all logical complexity will be a matter of the complexity of functional expressions. This leads to a distinction between the extensional identity of a propositional component associated with its *reference (Bedeutung)* and the logical or intensional identity associated with its *sense (Sinn)*. Two expressions are assigned the same sense if they can be substituted for one another in a proposition without affecting the validity of inferences containing it. The logical identity of a proposition can then be exhibited by a composition of the propositional sign. The functionalist view of logical complexity is *extensionalist* insofar as the truth-value of a proposition depends only on the extensional identity of its components and the manner of composition.

Among other things, that means that the logical principles are not about propositions or contents (thoughts) but about what gets quantified.[17] What

---

[15] Whatever may be appealing in such theories, they all face serious difficulties in accounting for the *unity* of the subjective and objective elements of judgment. Frege sees that this unity cannot be the same as the unity of a judgment's content. That is why, for example, though he glosses the internal unity of a judgment as "acknowledg[ing] the thought as true," he warns the reader against taking this acknowledgment as a further predication. Indeed, Frege denies that judgment can be defined at all, and speaks of its primitive unity, "something quite peculiar and incomparable" (Frege, "On Sinn and Bedeutung," in Michael Beaney, ed., *The Frege Reader,* trans. Max Black [Oxford: Blackwell, 1997], 159).

[16] Russell's conception of logic, in contrast, is *universalist* but not extensionalist or functionalist. In his framework logical principles range over propositions; functions are introduced by reference to propositional complexity—which is thus more basic than functional complexity.

[17] The quantifiers range over everything without restriction, though they fall into different types corresponding to the different types of functions. (Fregean quantifiers can range over objects, properties, or relations.)

distinguishes them from the principles of a special science is that they do not involve any topic-specific or genus-specific expressions.[18,19]

But Frege distinguishes three notions of *logical principles:*

(I) *Laws of truth*—thoughts expressed by generalizations free of any genus-specific concept-expressions. These truths, that ought to be asserted, are rendered apparent by the propositional signs of the *Begriffsschrift,* and are thus asserted by competent users of the *Begriffsschrift.*

(II) *Laws of thought*—principles of inference which are rational requirements or permissions pertaining to judgment in general (e.g., *modus ponens*). These principles are meant to be employed by any user of the *Begriffsschrift* in the assessments of her own reasoning.

(III) *Laws of holding true*—generalizations of empirical psychology that describe "historical" regularities among episodes of judging.[20] These

---

[18] Having such generality can only be a necessary condition for being a logical principle.

[19] Aristotle is sometimes read as an *extensionalist.* The idea is that the special sciences study "that which is" insofar as all quantifiers are unrestricted—just as first philosophy does, but in a different way. Here is Michael Wedin:

> So the special sciences satisfy universally quantified formulae—physics studies *any x* insofar as *x* has an internal principle of rest and motion, biology studies *any x* insofar as *x* has the capacity for living, and so on.
> The general science of being does not, then, differ formally from the special sciences, at least as so far characterized. It also studies that which is, and, like them, it does so under a specification that fixes its domain. But the specification in question is rather different. . . . [T]he general science of being studies things simply insofar as they *are,* that is, it studies any *x* insofar as *x* is. (M. Wedin, "The Science and Axioms of Being," in G. Anagnostopoulos, ed., *The Blackwell Companion to Aristotle,* 126)

By contrast, an *intensionalist* reading of Aristotle distinguishes what holds of something *essentially* from what does not. A special science would study the principles and attributes that hold of beings in virtue of some particular essence—for example, physics studies the principles and attributes that hold of natural beings in virtue of an internal principle of rest and motion. First philosophy would be the study of instances of being insofar as they are instances of being.

The problem is that—as we have seen—*being* in general does not have a particular essence. It is not clear, then, what first philosophy is supposed to be about. In Chapter 2 I shall suggest that this problem shows that the solution must lie in the recognition of the *syncategorematic.*

[20] In empirical psychology, unlike other sciences, generalizations involve the specification of content and thus the use of expressions in intensional contexts.

laws generalize over historical occurrences of the form '. . . . judges / believes ___ .'

Thus, the laws of thought pertain to a logical notion of judgment as an act expressed by assertion, whereas the laws of holding true generalize over judgments in the empirical sense which are ascribed by psychological-verbs in indirect discourse.[21]

OPNC turns out to be a law of truth, since it is put in terms of conjunctions, negations, and quantifiers over objects and properties, she who understands those expressions recognizes that she must acknowledge the truth of the thought expressed by this proposition; PPNC turns out to be a law of holding true and therefore a statement of a psychological fact with which one can agree or disagree.

As I mentioned, the dualist also recognizes a normative law of thought:

(NPNC) One ought not believe (judge) that the same thing is and is not.

NPNC, which we can call the *normative principle of noncontradiction*, is supposed to rest on OPNC considered as a law of truth, together with the principles of inference. A failure to respect it will be a failure to conform to an ideal. That does not mean it is *impossible;* logic cannot rule it out as impossible since the truth or falsity of "A judges that p" and "A judges that not-p" or even of "A judges that (p and not-p)" is an empirical psychological issue.

The logical difference between OPNC and PPNC reflects this distinction. The thought expressed by $\sim(p$ and $\sim p)$ is a logical truth and thus ought to be asserted; the thought expressed by $\sim$(A believes p and A believes $\sim p$) is not.

The dualist theory of judgment draws support from two observations.

---

[21] The distinction was recently described by Maria Van der Schaar in her "Frege on Judging and the Judging Agent," *Mind*, 2017 (https://doi.org/10.1093/mind/fzw059). Van der Schaar describes, convincingly, the first personal character of the logical notion of judgment as a key to Frege's logical work. The logical-psychological duality of judgments, and thus of the logical "I" and the empirical thinker, belongs together with the dualist account of the logical notion of judgment.

2.3.1.

The first is that simple affirmation and denial are related as affirmative and negative answers to a "yes-no" question. First the Stoics, and later Descartes, try to capture this observation by construing affirmation and denial as contrasting assessments of one representation (*lekta* or idea). To assent is to assess the representation as true; to dissent is to assess it as false. I will call this conception of judgment *Descartes's point*.

Since a representation is supposed to be truth-assessable independent of our actual assessment, assent and dissent cannot be construed as further representational acts—otherwise they too would have to be assessable as true or false, and so on. Descartes concludes that a judgment consists in a *nonrepresentational* act of will in relation to an idea received in the understanding.[22] But it is unclear why acts of will and understanding—which have turned out to be so different from one another—can both be called "mental." Michael Della Rocca, who raises this question, answers that "Descartes would certainly invoke what he sees as the defining feature of the mental, consciousness."[23] But Della Rocca also notes that this does not go far enough, "for we now inevitably ask: in virtue of what are the idea or volition both consciousness? And in virtue of what is the bodily state not consciousness?" He concludes: "[T]here is no natural answer to this question on Cartesian terms" (p. 151).

This failure reveals the precritical character of Descartes's notion of consciousness, which dissociates the unity of a judgment from the consciousness of that unity.

2.3.2.

The second observation is—as Geach puts it—that:

> a proposition may occur in discourse now asserted, now unasserted, and yet be recognizably the same proposition.[24]

---

[22] It seems to follow that a judgment is an intentional act, something one can choose to do. Later we shall see that this reflects a failure to distinguish the categorematic from the syncategorematic.

[23] Michael Della Rocca, "Judgment and Will," in Stephen Gaukroger, ed., *The Blackwell Guide to Descartes' Meditation* (Oxford: Blackwell, 2006), 150–151.

[24] Peter Geach, "Assertion," reprinted in *Logic Matters* (London: Basil Blackwell, 1972), 254–255.

Geach describes this observation as Frege's point, however, we shall see that this statement is open to different interpretation than the one Geach gives of it, and so in order to distinguish the statement from his specific reading of it I shall refer to it as *Frege's observation.*

It is worth noting that Geach is not using the term *proposition* in the Fregean sense of a *thought* or *content,* but rather, as he puts it elsewhere, "in a sense inherited from medieval logic, a bit of language identifiable in a certain recognizable logical employment."[25] It is a bit of *language*—but not just a "string of words." Different occurrences of the same words are recognizable as occurrences of the same proposition only within the larger logical context. (This is also what I mean when I talk of propositions and propositional signs.)[26]

The use of the term *occur* in Frege's observation is ambiguous between occurrence understood as the actual concrete occurrence of a propositional sign and a symbolic occurrence of a propositional sign within a larger propositional or logical context.

Geach assumes that the repeated occurrence of a proposition mentioned by Frege's observation lies within the context of valid arguments, and that the observation is implicit in the recognition of the validity of those arguments. For instance, we shall not understand how q can be validly inferred from (1) p and (2) if p then q if we do not see that p occurs in (1) as asserted and in (2) as unasserted. Geach agrees with Frege that we identify an argument as valid by recognizing it to be in accord with a principle of inference which is a norm that pertains to acts. Thus, on Geach's reading Frege's observation applies both to an actual argument of the form modus ponens and to modus ponens as a principle of inference. Therefore, Geach's understanding of Frege's observation conflates the two senses of propositional occurrence: symbolic and actual. Frege also runs these two senses together by introducing the judgment stroke as a logical symbol that indicates actual assertoric force, and that plays an essential role in the formulation of the principles of inference.

Understood as a point concerning a proposition's concrete occurrences it is the straightforward insight that having the character of an actual assertion, by contrast to having a semantical or logical identity, is characteristic of particular occurrences of a proposition that cannot be associated with the

[25] Peter Geach, "Kinds of Statements," in *Intention and Intentionality: Essays in Honor of Elizabeth Anscombe* (Ithaca, NY: Cornell University Press, 1979).

[26] "Etymologically," Geach reminds us, " 'proposition' suggests something propounded or put forward" ("Assertion," 254–255).

repeatable symbol. In other words, a propositional sign manifests, through its symbolic composition, the semantical character of each actual occurrence of the proposition, but not the force character of any those occurrences.

However, for Frege and Geach the observation amounts to something different. They want to say that anything within the composition of a propositional sign which is associated with assertoric force must be dissociated from that which carries semantic significance—that is, from *everything* directly relevant to its truth-value. In particular, they want to dissociate assertoric force from anything in the composition or form of that which is primarily true or false in a propositional sign.[27]

In what follows, I shall call the correct understanding of Frege's observation *Wittgenstein's point,* and I shall call the conclusion Geach and Frege draw from it—that assertoric force must be dissociated from a proposition's semantical significance—*Frege's point.* We shall see that Frege's point is mistaken. It only seems necessary if we accept certain functionalist (and more generally, compositionalist) assumptions about logical complexity. Correctly understood as Wittgenstein's point, Frege's observation concerns actual occurrences of a proposition and amounts to the full context principle; misunderstood as Frege's point it runs together the symbolic and actual occurrences of a proposition and limits the context principle to atomic propositions.

2.4.

In the *Begriffsschrift* Frege introduces a special symbol to indicate assertoric force—or more precisely, a symbol whose occurrence typically (but defeasibly) manifests assertion. Given Frege's point, this symbol must be external to the semantically significant composition of the proposition. Moreover, a

---

[27] For Geach, Frege's observation is meant to be restricted to occurrences of propositions in logical contexts that are identifiable as extensional or truth-functional. But understood as Wittgenstein's point, Frege's observation is not limited to a truth-functional context, and it implies semantic innocence, *p* is the same in *p* and in *A thinks p.* An expression of a generalized version of Frege's observation, one that assimilates intensional and extensional contexts, can be found in the following note from Wittgenstein's *Notes on Logic*:

> When we say A judges that, etc., then we have to mention a whole proposition which A judges. It will not do to mention only its constituents, or its constituents and form but not in the proper order. This shows that a proposition itself must occur in the statement to the effect that it is judged. For instance, however "not- p" may be explained, the question "What is negated?" must have a meaning. (96)

proposition that contains the symbol can only stand alone. It cannot be embedded as the significant constituent of a proposition.

Evidently Frege thinks that he needs the assertion symbol to exhibit the logical dependence of a conclusion on premises in valid inferences. But why?

Before I can answer this question I need to say a little more about the assertion symbol. Here is a passage from Frege's *Grundgesetze:*

> We have already said that in a mere equation there is as yet no assertion; "2 + 3 = 5" only designates a truth-value, without its being said which of the two it is. . . . We therefore require another special sign to be able to assert something as true. For this purpose I let the sign "⊢" precede the name of the truth-value, so that for example in "⊢2 + 2 = 4," it is asserted that the square of 2 is 4. I distinguish the judgment from the thought in this way: by a judgment I understand the acknowledgment of the truth of a thought. The presentation in Begriffsschrift of a judgment by use of the sign "⊢" I call a proposition of Begriffsschrift or briefly a proposition. I regard this "⊢" as composed of the vertical line, which I call the judgment-stroke, and the horizontal line, which I will now simply call the horizontal. . . . Of the two signs of which "⊢" is composed, only the judgment-stroke contains the act of assertion. (*The Basic Laws of Arithmetic*, 37–39)

The assertion symbol is a composite. But unlike every other composite sign in the *Begriffsschrift,* the composition of this symbol is not itself functional. The nature of its composition remains mysterious. Presumably it is unanalyzable in the same sense that "acknowledgment of something as true" is unanalyzable.

In any case, the assertion symbol combines the horizontal and the vertical. The horizontal is a first-order function-expression that has only the truth-value "true" in its extension. Apparently, its job is to mark, within the syntax of the *Begriffsschrift,* those complete expressions which have thoughts as their content. (It turns out that each expression that has a thought as its content has a counterpart with the same sense prefixed by the horizontal. In other words, the horizontal is *sense-transparent* when the sense of its argument is a thought.)[28]

---

[28] In the *Tractatus* Wittgenstein says:

> The verb of a proposition is not "is true" or "is false," as Frege thought: rather, that which "is true" must already contain the verb. (4.063)

The vertical is supposed to manifest assertion—the actuality of the act—and so is associated directly with assertoric force. It can be used only in connection with the horizontal, but that is not a *functional* application. (By contrast, logical connectives such as negation are introduced as functional modifications of the horizontal.) It follows that the vertical is external to the functional composition of the propositional sign, and thus to its semantically significant logical composition.

The horizontal is so to speak the vessel for the activity that the vertical infuses it with. But of course the horizontal can occur without this infusion. It can be embedded in logical connectives. In such cases we can say that it *displays* a judgment or an assertion with a certain content, or that it *manifests* the assertability of content.[29]

The distinction between a *display* and a *self-identifying display*, though it is not in Frege, can help us understand his distinction between the horizontal and the vertical. We say that a sample displays a repeatable. For example, Pantone #15–5519 displays turquoise. But not every sample has to be an *instance* of the repeatable. We can display *swimming* without actually swimming (e.g., by performing certain gestures on dry land). In this case the gestures display an act of a certain kind by means of its characteristic appearance without being an instance of the act. In contrast, a color sample is a self-identifying display, insofar as it is an instance of the very color it displays.

With this in mind, we can say that the completed horizontal displays an act—some assertion;[30] the vertical makes this a self-identifying display, at least under normal conditions (the horizontal by itself already manifests *assertability*—but that is not yet to manifest an actual assertion.)

Since the vertical does not belong to the functional composition of a proposition, it has no referential import. This distinguishes it, within the *Begriffsschrift*, as the sole *syncategorematic* expression. The whole symbol governed by a judgment-stroke, for example, " ⊢*p*," is itself a syncategorematic unit

---

The horizontal (or its negation) can be seen as the sole *verb* of a *Begriffsschrift* proposition, for it is the locus of assertability in a proposition. Frege splits the ordinary predicate into a locus of assertability and a locus of truth / falsity.

[29] We can call the horizontal the truth-predicate of the *Begriffsschrift* as long as we do not confuse it with the familiar semantic notion of predication that belongs to the schematic conception of logic.

[30] In some cases, e.g.,—(*p* and not-*p*), Frege wants us to regard the assertion displayed by the horizontal as an absurdity—that is, as pragmatically impossible.

since it cannot be embedded as a functional or predicative component within a logically complex whole. (In particular, it cannot be either a subject or a predicate term in a proposition.) As such, it cannot be repeated in different logical contexts, but can only stand by itself.

By contrast, we can say that in Frege's work any complete or incomplete expression is *categorematic,* since it is embeddable in a functional composite.

The *categorematic/syncategorematic* difference will emerge as the major concern of this work. But at this point it can be described simply as the difference between expressions that can and cannot be functionally embedded as part of a larger significant expression. For example, in the *Begriffsschrift* "-*p*" is a categorematic propositional sign because it can occur as a subordinate expression within a compound proposition. And, as I already mentioned, "⊢*p*" is a syncategorematic propositional sign.

To return to our question: Why does Frege think he needs the assertion symbol and its constituents?

The answer has to do with Frege's point. The business of logic, as Frege understands it, is to construct a notation *(Begriffsschrift)* that exhibits the unity of valid inferences through the composition of propositional signs. As I mentioned, Frege's main conviction was that, if the validity of an inference from a generalization to its instance is put in terms of quantified propositions, the semantically significant composition of a propositional sign will be that of a functional expression.

But an inference, Frege says, is an act governed by *norms:* rational requirements or permissions to perform one act (of assertion, judgment, etc.) on the basis of others. It follows from Frege's point that the principles of inference are not laws of truth. Nonetheless, these principles are essential to logic. And the assertion symbol is clearly essential to *them.* Take Frege's specification of *modus ponens* in the *Grundgesetze:*

> From the propositions "⊢ Δ implies Γ" and "⊢ Δ" we can infer: "⊢ Γ." (§14, *The Basic Laws of Arithmetic*)

Not: *it follows,* but: *we can—we are permitted—to infer.*

2.5.

In his later work Frege will speak of *assertoric form* rather than the judgment-stroke.

We express acknowledgement of truth in the form of an assertoric sentence. We do not need the word "true" for this. And even when we do use it the properly assertoric force does not lie in it, but in the assertoric sentence-form; and where this form loses its assertoric force, the word "true" cannot put it back again. ("Thought," in Michael Beaney, ed., *The Frege Reader*, trans. P. Geach and R. H Stoothoff [Oxford: Blackwell, 1997], 330)

In other words, an utterance in ordinary language with "the form of an assertoric sentence" will typically (but defeasibly) constitute an assertion.

The implication is that "acknowledging the truth of a thought"—judging it to be true—is not a further predication. Assertoric form can only be *syncategorematic* since it does not belong to the functional composition of a proposition.

We might wonder how this gets conveyed in ordinary language. There are of course indicative mood-markers—grammatical mechanisms for distinguishing declarative from interrogative or imperative sentences. But these are not enough. Assertoric form cannot be embedded within logically compound sentences. Indicative mood-markers can be.[31]

Written language seems to offer additional resources—as Geach points out:

In written or printed language, there is a certain presumption—though of course it can be upset in various ways—that an author of a nonfictional work intends a sentence to be read as an assertion if it stands by itself between full stops and grammatically can be read as an assertion. The assertoric force of a sentence is thus shown by its not being enclosed in the context of a longer sentence. ("Assertion," 162)

Suppose then that a written indicative sentence, together with the appropriate punctuation, makes up a syncategorematic unit analogous to '*p*' (or to an utterance of an indicative sentence followed by short silence).

It is clear even this is only a rule of thumb. A proposition can never lose its content, or its semantical character. But—as Frege says—a sentence *can* "lose its assertoric force," since in certain settings the force is somehow upset.

---

[31] The indicative mood-marker might be thought of as analogous to Frege's horizontal. But the analogy is problematic. The horizontal is supposed to belong to a proposition's functional form, while Frege seems to deny that the indicative mood-marker has functional significance.

Or in my terminology: it is *displayed* but is no longer an instance of what it displays; it is not a self-identifying display.

Frege writes:

> The truth claim arises in each case from the form of the assertoric sentence, and when the latter lacks its usual force, e.g., in the mouth of an actor upon the stage, even the sentence "The thought that 5 is a prime number is true" contains only a thought and even the same thought as the simple "5 is a prime number." ("On Sense and Reference," in *The Frege Reader*, 158)

This example is supposed to show that "where this form loses its assertoric force, the word 'true' cannot put it back again." But it is also supposed to corroborate Frege's point. For if a thought can be conveyed without assertoric force, assertoric form must be external to a proposition's semantical character.

But we do not have to say that a thought can be conveyed without assertoric force. The actors in a play *do* display assertions. The actor who says, "I am thy father's spirit, / Doom'd for a certain term to walk the night," displays the assertion that he is Hamlet's father's spirit. It is just that, by convention, the display of assertion *in a play* is not an assertion but a *mock* assertion.

I want to suggest that a similar point applies to logic. In the theater the display of force is not an assertion; the setting upsets the force-form. In a compound proposition too, the display of force is not an assertion. Here too—I suggest—the setting upsets the force-form, which is nonetheless displayed. If that is right, then we do not have to infer Frege's point from Frege's observation, or conflate Wittgenstein's point with Frege's point. We can say instead that predicative form *does* display force—but that not all such displays are in fact assertions.

This is what I *will* say. In what follows, I will argue that Frege is wrong to distinguish the manifestation of assertability by predicative propositions from the manifestation of a significant logical unity. (In fact they coincide.) In other words, he is wrong to distinguish the display of assertoric force from the manifestation of a logical unity which constitutes something as being true or false.

2.6.

In *The Foundations of Arithmetic* Frege outlines three main commitments of his logical work:

(1) To separate sharply the psychological from the logical, the subjective from the objective.

(2) To ask after the meaning of the word only in the context of a proposition, not in isolation.

(3) To keep in mind the distinction between concept and object. (trans. J. L. Austin [Oxford: Blackwell, 1974], x)

And he indicates that these commitments are so united that a violation of one implies a violation of the others.[32]

Later I will suggest that these commitments can be seen as foreshadowing the *syn/categorematic* difference.[33] At this point I want to note that Frege's own logic violates all three commitments.

---

[32] We can see this if we consider how traditional syllogistic violates these principles. A syllogism is an inference whose premises and conclusion are propositions composed of subject and predicate terms of the form "All (some, no) *A*s are (not) *B*s." The premises contain just three terms, the "middle" of which can occur first as subject and then as predicate positions. In general, then, syllogistic logic does not recognize a categorial difference between expressions that occur in these positions. Every syllogistic term must have an extension—must signify a concept in Frege's sense. And this violates commitment (3).

From Frege's point of view the traditional syllogistic also disregards the distinction between predicates and singular terms, since it treats singular terms as general terms and general terms as names. For example, it treats "Socrates is mortal" as equivalent to "All Socrateses are mortal"—otherwise it could not be the premise or conclusion of a syllogism.

Since a proposition, so understood, cannot represent an individual as belonging to the extension of a term, the semantic relation of a term to its extension must be grasped apart from the context of the proposition. This violates Frege's commitment (2), the context principle.

And, Frege adds:

> If the second principle is not observed, one is almost forced to take as the meaning of words as mental pictures or acts of individual minds and so to offend against the first principle as well. (*Foundations of Arithmetic*, trans J. L. Austin [Oxford: Basil Blackwell, 1950], x)

In traditional logic a term is supposed to be grasped through *abstraction* from experience. But this is a subjective act, and so it violates commitment (1).

[33] In Chapter 2 the psycho/logical distinction in (1) will turn out to be a shadow of the syn/categorematic difference itself; the context principle in (2) will turn out to be a shadow of the syncategorematic unity of a predicative proposition; the concept/object distinction in (3) will turn out to be a shadow of the singular-term/verb difference internal to the predicative.

Commitment (1)—"to separate sharply the psychological from the logical"—is an injunction against confusing anything manifested by the logical symbolism with subjective episodes or states (ideas, sensations, etc.). But Frege violates this injunction by admitting the judgment / assertion stroke into his logic, since its role is to manifest the actual act of assertion and so it is external to the significant functional composition of a proposition.

Commitment (2) is known as the *context principle*. The idea is that the semantical difference between two expressions is the difference made by substituting one for the other in a proposition. Conversely, the parts of a proposition are revealed by the broader logical context in which it occurs. For Frege that means *inferences,* which he conceives along psycho / logical dualist lines—as the making of one judgment on the basis of others—is subject to certain logical norms.

The implication is that the expressions which make up a simple proposition cannot play one logical role in some of their occurences and another role in others. In particular, a self-standing expression cannot *also* figure, in other contexts, as a logical constituent of a proposition.

But this shows that commitment (2) applies only to the expressions that make up simple propositions. By contrast, a proposition can occur by itself or as a component in a compound proposition. That is: they can occur as asserted or unasserted ("Frege's point"). Frege's context principle is in fact limited to atomic propositions. Hence, atomic propositions enjoy semantic autonomy relative to the larger context in which they occur as components. The limitation of the context principle is a consequence of the functionalist's univocal notion of logical complexity, which does not allow for a sharp distinction between the sense in which a name occurs in an atomic proposition, and the sense in which an atomic proposition occurs in a compound proposition.

Finally, (3) is a commitment to separate the particular from the general. Traditional syllogistic fails here, according to Frege, because it does not distinguish names from general terms. One purpose of his symbolic treatment of quantification is to capture this distinction.

According to Frege a nonassertoric propositional sign is composed by the application of a functional expression to one or more arguments or expressions. The difference between a singular term (or name) and a predicate is supposed to consist in the difference between a special kind of first-level functional expression (a concept-expression) and the expressions that *complete* or *saturate* its empty argument place.

But the account fails. It cannot mark predicates (i.e., concept-words) as distinct from first-order functional expressions. For example, it cannot mark the difference between a functional expression such as *the capital of . . .* and a concept-word such as *. . . is wise.* There is thus an irony in the very title *Begriffsschrift,* since its notation fails to capture the distinctive logical character of a concept *(Begriff).*

In fact the mark of a predicate is simply that it is *negatable:* it has a contradictory counterpart. As we shall see, this is connected with Aristotle's insight, in *De Interpretatione,* that the verb in a simple proposition has the job of *asserting* something. In denying this—in separating assertoric force from the concept-word—Frege loses the resources to distinguish concept-words as negatable expressions from nonnegatable functional expressions.[34]

2.7.

The textbook account of truth-functional propositional complexity begins from Frege's point. A compound proposition is built up by the application of a truth-functional proposition-forming connective—the *governing connective*—to a sequence of one or more subordinate propositions. The truth-value of the whole is said to be a function of the truth-values of the components in relation to the governing connective.

In such an account, we start with a notion of the values *true* and *false* as contrary features of simple propositions, and extend this notion to include compound propositions. Hence, on such an account, a simple proposition has its truth-value independently of the contribution it makes to the truth-value of the compound propositions in which it occurs. In

---

[34] Frege thinks he can get around the problem with the horizontal (the content-stroke). An incomplete functional expression would be negatable just in case it is prefixed by the horizontal. But this construal of concept expressions rests on an incoherent association of the unity of a contradictory pair of assertions with the duality of truth and falsehood, understood as two objects with contrary properties (see TLP 4.063).

accordance with Frege's point, the subordinate propositions must be logically self-contained units within the compound. It follows that logically equivalent propositions may not have equivalent senses. Take for example the propositions p and $\sim\sim p$. Evidently these are logically equivalent. Nonetheless, for Frege they must have different logical identities, since the first but not the second contains $\sim p$. Therefore, since the truth of one, but not the other, depends on the value of $\sim p$ they must have different senses.

Since the subordinate propositions in a compound are treated as logical building blocks, so to speak, I will call this a *spatio-logical account* of truth-functional propositional complexity.[35]

Spatio-logicism appears to be the consequence of the observation that a simple proposition can stand by itself and as the logical component of a compound proposition. This observation appears to show that the context principle does not apply to the components of a compound proposition. Hence it appears that we can ask how the truth-value of a simple predicative proposition is determined in isolation from the context of compound propositions in which it can occur as a component. But we shall find that the monistic treatment of logical complexity rejects this implication. The monistic understanding of the proposition will reveal that even though a simple predicative proposition can occur alone, we cannot ask for its meaning in isolation from the propositional contexts in which it can occur. The monist's context principle can be described as *complete* or *full* by contrast to the Fregean context principle that applies only to the components of simple predicative propositions.

---

[35] G. E. M. Anscombe uses the term "logical chemistry" to describe such an account:

> Consider the explanations of propositions and truth-functions, or logical constants, which are commonly found in logic books. It is usual for us to be told: first, propositions are whatever can be either true or false; second, propositions can be combined in certain ways to form further propositions; and third, in examining these combinations, i.e., in developing the truth-functional calculus, we are not interested in the internal structure of the combined propositions. . . . [I]s there not an impression as it were of *logical chemistry* about these explanations? (*An Introduction to Wittgenstein's* Tractatus [New York: Harper & Row, 1965], 53)

Anscombe correctly rejects a reading of the *Tractatus* that ascribes to it this "logical chemistry." My suggestion is that the main features of such an account arise from Frege's point.

2.8.

In *The Principles of Mathematics,* Bertrand Russell treats judgment as a relation between the judging subject and a complex entity, the object of judgment, which he calls a *proposition.* (This is a form of psycho/logical dualism.) He denies that the truth of a proposition can be defined in terms of the truth of another proposition in which it appears as a term ("term" being his word for propositional constituents), for such a definition would be hopelessly circular. Instead, he says, a proposition must be semantically self-contained. Its truth-value depends only on what is internal to it. Consequently, propositions and their constituents are not representations, but elements of reality.

What unites a proposition is an *activity* which is associated with the term that occurs in it as a verb. Russell describes this activity as an *assertion* in a nonpsychological sense. Here the word *nonpsychological* indicates that the activity is not added to a proposition by the judging subject, but is immanent to it. For example, the proposition "Desdemona loves Othello" is united by the verb *love.* But the example also shows the problem with this treatment. Since the proposition is supposed to consist in the *actual* relation of its constituents, its mere being amounts to its truth. Not only falsehood, but all propositional complexity—including negation—is thus unintelligible.

To address this problem Russell draws a distinction between asserted and unasserted propositions.

> [I]f I may be allowed to use the word *assertion* in a non-psychological sense the proposition "*p* implies *q*" asserts an implication, though it does not *assert* *p* or *q*. (B. Russell, *Principles of Mathematics* [Cambridge: Cambridge University Press, 1903], §38)

Since it now belongs to the logical identity of a proposition that it is an assertion, Russell cannot accept Frege's observation that (in Geach's summary) "a proposition may occur in discourse now asserted, now unasserted, and yet be recognizably the same proposition." Although asserted propositions are distinguished from unasserted propositions by their intrinsic character, Russell cannot say what the distinction is. But—he adds—"Leaving the puzzle to logic . . . we must insist that there is a difference of some kind between asserted and unasserted propositions."

Because Russell's treatment of propositions does not accommodate Frege's observation, it cannot recognize the logical form of contradictory pairs or the form of valid inferences such as *modus ponens.*

Frege's treatment does accommodate his observation—but only by denying that the repeatable expression of the thought *p* is intrinsically assertable. But since, as we have seen, his conception of logic requires a symbolic mark of assertoric force—the judgment-stroke—an assertoric proposition *p* manifests the internal division between its assertoric form and its functionally significant composition.

2.9.

In one of his notebooks, Wittgenstein says:

> Assertion is merely psychological. In not-*p*, *p* is exactly the same as if it stands alone; this point is absolutely fundamental. (*Notebooks 1914–1916*, 95)

I do not think this should be read as a demand for a purer dualism, a purer separation of assertion from logic. Instead, I will argue, it is a rejection of the psycho / logical dualism in both Russell *and* Frege. It is a statement of psycho / logical monism.

The point is that neither Russell nor Frege can adequately accommodate Frege's observation, that: "In not-*p*, *p* is exactly the same as if it stands alone." Russell denies that asserted and unasserted propositions have the same character, while Frege thinks that insofar as *p* can both stand alone and occur in not-*p*, it is not subject to the context principle, which means that we can ask for the meaning of *p* in isolation from its occurrence in -*p*.

I would argue that the monist accommodates the observation by recognizing, first, that we identify *p* as a repeatable that can occur alone and in -*p* by reference to the unity of the contradictory pair, and second, that this unity depends, in turn, on the repeatability of a propositional sign. For the monist a propositional sign *p*, though it can stand alone, is subject to the full context principle. Hence, we can say that logic, according to the monist, is internal to simple predicative signs.

We need to ask what Wittgenstein means by "psychology" when he describes assertion as "merely psychological." While both Frege and Russell distinguish assertion in the psychological sense (as a propositional attitude) from assertion in the logical or non-psychological sense, Wittgenstein rejects this distinction by insisting that the *p* in not-*p* and also in *A judges p* is exactly the same as *p* standing alone. One may wonder, however, why Wittgenstein says that assertion is psychological rather than logical, especially since he associates assertion with the unity of a proposition.

The answer lies in our distinction between *displaying* an assertion and *being* an assertion. The display is of a repeatable: a concrete occurrence of a propositional sign is a display of a repeatable act. This display can be either an assertion (a self-identifying display) or a *gesture* (a mere display).

Wittgenstein's remark suggests that logical unities, for example, of *p* and not-*p*, are internal to the repeatability of signs and are therefore manifested by the symbolism. The rest—the features of concrete propositional occurrences that are not manifested in the symbolism—come under the heading of psychology. And Wittgenstein's point implies that being an *assertion—the actuality of assertion*—is such a feature.

This way of distinguishing the logical from the psychological is quite unlike those introduced earlier. It belongs to psycho / logical monism.

2.10.

I take Wittgenstein to be a thoroughgoing psycho / logical monist. Even when he changes his mind about other things, he never changes his mind about *that*.

The notion that logic is not concerned with actual, historical occurrences of linguistic expressions but only with symbolical occurrences of expressions within larger symbolical contexts lies at the heart of Wittgenstein's early work. Later he would note, for example, that the common or regular agreement between speakers in what they describe by the use of the predicate "... *F*," is not logically external to the assertoric act of describing something as "... *F*." And he insists that, in saying this, we do not lose the integrity of logic—we do not give in to psycho-logicism.[36]

---

[36] Compare *Philosophical Investigations* §242:

> If language is to be a means of communication there must be agreement not only in definition but also (queer as this sounds) in judgments. This seems to abolish logic, but does not do so. It is one thing to describe a method of measurement, and another to obtain and state results of measurement. But what we call "measuring" is partly determined by a certain constancy in results of measurement.

The remark seems addressed to his own earlier separation of logic and psychology.

This is an important development in his thought. But it falls entirely within the framework of psycho / logical monism.[37]

3. Psycho / Logical Monism

3.1.

Psycho / logical monism accommodates Kant's insight that a judgment belongs to a certain context of activity: the activity whose unity is the same as the consciousness of its unity, or self-consciousness. According to Kant, a judgment is a certain unity of consciousness. As such, it is a capacity for identifying consciousness as having this unity; but in saying that that one should be careful not to confuse an "act of identifying consciousness" with subsumption under a general kind, namely, with a determination of consciousness.[38]

Frege also says that a judgment belongs to a larger context—the context of valid inference. But there is an important difference from Kant. According to Frege, the unity of inference—understood as a norm-governed activity— is independent of the consciousness of that unity. This is why a *Begriffsschrift* is needed. For Kant the clarification of an activity in self-consciousness already belongs to the logical context of judgment, since the context *just is* (in capacity) self-consciousness.

A fundamental difference between the monistic and dualistic conceptions of logic is that in the former but not in the latter the "I" is a logical word on a level with the logical connectives. For the monist, the unity expressed by the connective is the unity of self-consciousness.

According to Kant, the judgment "*p*" is the same as the first-personal ascription of that judgment ("I think *p*"). This sameness is not an *identity*. If

---

[37] Even so, Wittgenstein's earlier view of logic—as the study of a capacity independent of its actualizations—exhibits a sort of vestigial dualism. His later view develops out of a deeper understanding of monism.

[38] According to Kant, consciousness as a whole (synthetic unity) is implicit in any unity in consciousness. The unity of consciousness is thus prior to the unity of any constituent of consciousness. But any unity in consciousness is also a self-conscious identification of consciousness in terms of a repeatable (analytic unity). The critical insight recognizes the sameness of the synthetic and analytic unities.

"*p*" is an utterance of consciousness, "I think *p*" is an utterance of *self-consciousness* (and "*p*"). It is not an identity, since "I think *p* or I think not-*p*" is not a tautology, while "*p* or not-*p*" is. Nonetheless, "I think" does not add any *content* to consciousness. "I think *p*" is already implicit in the consciousness that contains "*p*."

Consciousness so understood is an *act of unity* through the self-consciousness of that unity. This act is at the same time a *capacity* for spontaneous expansion by self-clarifications that are self-ascriptions—that is, by the employment of "I." The description of consciousness as an *act* here might suggest that consciousness is a substance in Aristotle's sense: an activity *(energeia)* of maintaining the unity of a substance-form. But we shall see that this useful analogy is deceptive.

Because "I think" does not add any predicative determination (i.e., predicative content) to consciousness, self-consciousness is not the perception of an inner domain. We can say that spontaneous self-consciousness is a *classification* of consciousness—that is, a classification of consciousness as containing *p*. But it is not a predication that subsumes consciousness under a type; and in particular, the "I" of this logical self-consciousness does not single out a determinable being (a soul-substance).

Earlier I said that Aristotle is supposed to have derived PPNC from OPNC on the assumption that judgments inhere in the judging subject as its attributes; the *togetherness* of judgments in one consciousness (as in PPNC) is supposed to be the same as the *com-presence* of attributes in one bearer (as in OPNC).

What Kant brought to light is that a judgment does not inhere in consciousness as a property or relation. If we call it a *mode* of consciousness, then we do so in a radically different sense than we do a mode of substance: for the modes of consciousness are the same as the self-consciousness of these modes. They are ascribed only if they can be *self*-ascribed (through the "I" in its logical use).

Similarly, the togetherness of several judgments in one consciousness is radically different from the compresence of several properties in one bearer. The compresence of properties is generally independent of self-consciousness. But the impossibility of *thinking* contradictory judgments together is a matter of the self-consciousness of the *together*. Conversely, judging that *p* is inseparable from a consciousness of its agreement with whatever else I think.

3.2. Critical Fregeanism

There is a tendency in recent philosophy to put Frege's notion of *sense* in terms of a unity of consciousness. The idea is to give a quasi-Kantian logical treatment of object-dependent thought—we might call it *Critical Fregeanism*. But we shall see that it precludes a logical (syncategorematic) notion of the "I."[39]

Here is Gareth Evans:

> The sense of a sentence, which is of course a function of the sense of its parts, is (in Frege's terminology) a thought; and the single constraint Frege imposed upon his notion of thought was that it should conform to what we may call "the Intuitive Criterion of Difference," namely that the thought associated with one sentence *S* as its sense must be different from the thought associated with another sentence *S'* as *its* sense, if it is possible for someone to understand both sentences at a given time while coherently taking different attitudes towards them, i.e. accepting (rejecting) one while rejecting (accepting), or being agnostic about, the other. (*The Varieties of Reference* [Oxford: Clarendon Press, 1982], 18–19)

This is a psycho-logical criterion: a thought is identified by its incompossibility with certain judgments in one consciousness. That is plausible. But the criterion turns out to be incompatible with Frege's spatio-logicism, as a result, Critical Fregeanism is incoherent.

Consider two conjunctions:

(i) $p \& q$
(ii) $p \& \text{-}p$

---

[39] Frege's logical work aims to clarify a logical notion of judgment, one which is expressed by assertoric form in direct discourse. This is in contrast to the post-Fregean approaches we are dealing with here, which regards all judgments as propositional attitudes. Sebastian Rödl has shown that these post-Fregean dualistic approaches do not have an adequate conception of judgments, because they have no place for the logical use of "I." (See *Self-Consciousness and Objectivity: An Introduction to Absolute Idealism* [Cambridge, MA: Harvard University Press, 2018].) Frege's work cannot be subjected to the same critique since the logical use of "I" can be associated with the judgment stroke or with assertoric form. Frege's account of judgment must be rejected as inadequate, not because it gives no place for the logical "I," but because it logically dissociates two notions of judgment: my judgment, which is expressed by assertoric form, and the judgment I ascribe to others as propositional attitudes in indirect discourse.

From the Fregean point of view (i) and (ii) are composed of the same components, and hence, since (i) clearly expresses a thought, so too must (ii).

Since there is no spatio-logical restriction on judgment to prevent our acknowledging such a thought as true—or rejecting it as false—it follows that "*p* & *-p*" is a possible judgment.[40] If we can make this judgment, it follows that we can *coherently* take different attitudes to *p* at the same time. According to the Intuitive Criterion, then, *p* has a different sense than *p*! This result can be avoided if the notion of assertoric force is understood to exclude contents such as *p* & *-p*. But this will result in a monistic treatment of acts, since everything in logic will enter into the constitution of assertoric force.

Critical Fregeanism is Fregean because its notions of sense and force are designed to accommodate Frege's point. But a monistic treatment of compound propositions must reject Frege's point and the spatio-logical conception of propositional complexity that it necessarily implies. The monist will say that the propositional sign "*p* & *-p*" does not display any judgment. But that does not mean it is *dispensable*. It is a sign that reveals something important by displaying its own emptiness. It can be described as both internal and external to the language.

3.3.

The dualist thinks there must be a requirement on thinkers not to hold together a triad of judgments of the form: $< p \rightarrow q, p, -q >$.

The requirement is only called for because logic, according to the dualist, does not exclude *psychologically* impossible combinations. It is only a ground of requirements for self-consistancy; it cannot prevent us from violating them. This is what leads to the vicious regress of the Tortoise and Achilles.[41]

---

[40] Frege himself holds that "p and not-p" express a thought, but that on pain of pragmatic contradiction one cannot attach a judgment stroke to it, since by using the judgment stroke one manifests one's capacity to understand logical expressions. Hence, he describes such assertions as absurd rather than nonsensical:

> The assertion of a thought which contradicts a logical law can indeed appear, if not nonsensical, then at least absurd; for the truth of a logical law is immediately evident of itself, from the sense of the expression. But a thought which contradicts a logical law may be expressed since it may be negated. (Frege, "Compound Thoughts," in *Collected Papers on Mathematics, Logic, and Philosophy* [Oxford: Blackwell, 1984, 405)

[41] See Lewis Carroll, "What the Tortoise Said to Achilles," *Mind* 104, no. 416 (1895): 691–93.

For the monist the regress never begins. There is no logical distance to traverse from judging $< p \rightarrow q, p >$ to judging q. A triad of the form $< p \rightarrow q, p, \sim q >$ does not jointly determine a possible act in consciousness. In a sense, the judgment that $< p \rightarrow q, p > just is$ the judgment that q. In *what* sense it is I will try to explain.

From the point of view of monism, to assert that $p \rightarrow q$ is to express an identification of our consciousness, on the basis of the judgments displayed as p and q, as a consciousness in which p and $\sim q$ cannot co-inhere. This identification is based on a display of repeatable acts which does not occur in consciousness; yet it is not a *determination,* since the judgment $p \rightarrow q$ is simply a clarification of what already belongs to consciousness. (It is a "reflective" judgment.)

In general, logically compound assertions such as $p \rightarrow q$ are acts of identifying our consciousness as agreeing or disagreeing with the combination (and their negations) displayed by the subordinate judgments. These can be said to *display* an assertion without manifesting it.

As I mentioned earlier, I term any display of an assertion that is also an instance of an assertion *self-identifying.* Any display that is not self-identifying I call an *assertoric gesture.* An assertoric gesture is analogous to a *mimetic* gesture that displays an act without being it—as a stewardess in an airplane displays the use of a life jacket without using it. A mimetic gesture can be performed as a basis for another act, as when we threaten someone by tracing a finger slowly across our neck. Similarly, an assertoric gesture occurs as a basis for the display of another repeatable, for example, p in $\sim p$. An assertoric gesture is an occurrence of a repeatable—a propositional sign—that can occur either as a gesture or as a self-identifying display.

My suggestion is that p and q occur as assertoric gestures in the judgment $p \rightarrow q$.

Consider the following pair of assertions:

(1) p
(2) $\sim p$

The very same p occurs in (1) as in (2). In (1), p exemplifies the assertion it displays (it is self-identifying). In (2), it displays the assertion without exemplifying it (it is a gesture). The contradictory unity of (1) and (2) governs the assertion displayed by (1). But this unity depends on the repeatability of the propositional sign p. We must recognize, at one at the same time, the priority of the propositional sign p and the dominance of the contradictory unity of (1) and (2).

3.4.

Some consequences:

(1) Judging that p is the same as judging that I think p.

"I think p" can be called a *spontaneous self-clarification* of p. I call it self-clarificatory because it brings out the content of consciousness without adding anything to it or determining anything about it. I call it *spontaneous* because the clarification is immediately available through the display of the judgment that p.

(2) Judging both that p, and that q, is the same as judging p together with q.

This also implies that judging that p and judging that q are the same as judging that I think p & q.
    Finally,

(3) Disagreeing with p is the same as judging that $\sim p$.

For example, a consciousness that contains the judgment "this is blue" is one that disagrees with the judgment "this is red"; so it also contains the judgment "this is not red."
    We can make (1), (2), and (3) more precise by distinguishing judgments *in activity* from judgments *in spontaneous capacity*. A judgment is in spontaneous capacity when it is immediately available through a spontaneous act. A judgment is a capacity for the manifestation of consciousness through an assertion involving a display that is self-identifying. So:

(1*) Judging that p is the same as judging that I think p (in activity or spontaneous capacity).

(2*) Judging both that *p* and that *q* is the same as judging that *p* & *q* (in activity or spontaneous capacity), which is also the same as judging that I think *p* & *q* (in activity or spontaneous capacity).

(3*) Disagreeing with *p* is the same as judging that -*p* (in activity or spontaneous capacity).

3.5.

However it is formulated, the principle of noncontradiction must involve two logical connectives: *negation* and *conjunction*. Both are essential to self-consciousness. Conjunction is essential to the act of bringing several judgments together in one consciousness. This act cannot be expressed by a mere *list* of assertions one after another—for each item on the list might belong to a different state of consciousness.

Negation is essential to the act of identifying ourselves as disagreeing with a judgment. For example, it allows us to distinguish our consciousness from one that errs through the negated judgment.

Conjunction and negation are *reflective acts*. They mark the consciousness of judgment as self-conscious. ("I think" is another such act.) In this way, they are distinguished from predicating or determining an object *within* consciousness. In what follows I will call them *operations*.

3.6.

An operation is a way of identifying a state of consciousness on the basis of gestures. *Truth-operations* are self-conscious acts of identifying states of consciousness in terms of the conjunction and negation of judgments on the basis of assertoric gestures.

The result of a truth-operation is an identification of consciousness as combining some judgments and disagreeing with others. All truth-operations are thus constructible by repeated applications of negation to predicative judgments.

The negative judgment not-*p* is an application of the operation -(. . .) to the gesture *p;* -(. . .) is thus an identification of consciousness as disagreeing with the act displayed by the gesture; not-*p* is an identification of consciousness as disagreeing with *p*.

The operation (. . . &__) is an identification of consciousness as containing the acts displayed by different gestures. The judgment *p* & *q* is an identification of consciousness as containing both *p* and *q*, and so as disagreeing with any combination of judgments that contains either not-*p* or not-*q*.

All the other truth-operations can be defined in terms of conjunction and negation. For example, *p* → *q* can be defined as ~(*p* & ~*q*)—that is, in terms of a disagreement with the conjunction *p* & ~*q*.[42]

Not all operations are truth-operations. The ascription "A thinks *p*" is not a truth-operation, since it does not identify consciousness in terms of combination and disagreement. Nonetheless, "A thinks . . ." is an operation, and "A thinks *p*" places me in actual or possible agreement or disagreement with A in regard to *p*. The operation "A thinks . . ." together with the operations of truth and falsity assessments are in play in the syllogism of thinking and being. Since "A thinks . . ." is an operation here, A is not a subject of predicative determination or a relata of a relation (I will return to this.)

A compound proposition displays an assertion on the basis of predicative propositions. But the monist holds that the form of a compound proposition, such as a conjunction, is not itself predicative. Since negation in a simple predicative proposition is attracted to the predicate, it can seem that there is a difference between "simple" and "compound" negation—and a corresponding difference between "simple" and "compound" principles of noncontradiction. But we shall see that these differences are illusory. Predicative contradiction will turn out to be a case of propositional contradiction even though the primary form of negation is indeed "simple."

---

[42] Even though the identity sign does not have the surface appearance of an operation, I would propose that it nevertheless is a syncategorematic sign. I wish to leave open here whether, and how, it can be construed as an operation. But in any case, the claim "a = b" can be construed as constituting a consciousness for which the assertions of the form "*Fa*" and "~*Fb*" *are incompossible,* and according to which there is no simple proposition *p* such that is incompossible with both ~*Fb and Fa.* However, we can say that relative to the claim "a = b" a pair of the form < Fb, ~Fa > is "contradictory-like," without thereby being judgments that constitute a contradictory pair, since "A thinks *Fb and ~Fa*" is not ruled out as incompossible with "a = b." The claim "a = b" is neither merely metalinguistic, i.e., a claim merely about names, nor is it merely objective—a claim about the bearers of names.

3.7.

The problem for monism is to explain the unity and difference that makes the pair of judgments < *p,* not-*p* > contradictory—so that asserting one is the same as excluding the other—without dissociating force from sense. There are two kinds of dualist specifications of the contradictory pair. According to the first, which captures what I called Descartes's point, contradictory judgments agree in content but disagree in force; they consist of contrasting positive and negative assertoric acts—affirmation and denial. According to the second, which is based on Frege's point, contradictory judgments or assertions agree in force but have contents that are logically related as a thought and its negation. According to the first view, negation indicates force, whereas according to the second, the negation sign reflects the relation between propositional contents. Both views are based on the assumption that the primary locus of truth and falsity is identifiable independently of the unity of the contradictory pair of judgments. This is what the monist rejects as incoherent.

The challenge facing the monist account is to elucidate the unity and difference that make a pair of judgments or assertions a contradictory pair without the separation of force and content. This has to be done in a way that reveals that the unity of the contradictory pair is constitutive of the notions of truth and falsehood—in particular, the truth (or falsity) of one judgment in a pair must be *the same* as the falsity (or truth) of the other.

I propose that in order to elucidate the internal unity of the contradictory pair we are well advised to consider the notion of a *two-way capacity,* which Aristotle introduces in *Metaphysics* Theta 2. "As regards those capacities which are rational"—literally, *with reason, meta logou*—the very same capacity is a capacity for opposites, but as regards capacities without *logos,* a single capacity is for one thing: for example, heat only for heating, whereas medical craft is for both disease and health (*Meta.* Theta, 1046b).

A two-way capacity is a capacity both to *inform* and to *deform.* The very same understanding which is exercised in *informing* (say, healing) is also exercised in *deforming* (say, poisoning). This understanding is associated with a form, which can therefore be described as a *two-way form.* The two acts of a two-way capacity are not symmetrical. The positive act is prior to the negative, in the sense that the capacity is *directed toward* the positive or informing act. The negative or deforming act is therefore somehow deficient.

I want to suggest that judgment is also a two-way capacity: a *two-way logical* or *propositional capacity.* The positive and negative acts of this capacity comprise a contradictory pair. For example, the judgments *p* and not-*p* would be activities of the same capacity—a capacity to judge that *p*.

The capacity is asymmetrical since the negative act is based on the positive gesture. But both acts of the capacity are identified by their unity as logical acts in consciousness: it is the very same determination in each case. Frege's point is therefore false; so is the spatio-logical account of propositional complexity.

There are two important differences between the two-way capacities Aristotle describes in Theta 2 and the logical capacities I have been discussing.

First, propositional acts are not *intentional actions*. Generally speaking, doctors *choose* to practice medicine. They heal with a view to some end; they can poison with a view to some other end. But we do not *choose* to judge that *p*, or to judge that *p* with a view to some end.

And second, a capacity *meta logou* is *categorematic:* it is specified by a verb—say, *to heal*—and its positive and negative acts are *contraries*. A logical capacity is *syncategorematic:* it is specified by a proposition, and its positive and negative acts are *contradictories*.[43] The judgment that not-*p* simply reverses the syncategorematic direction displayed in *p*.

But this notion of a *syncategorematic* or logical two-way capacity is just what we need to understand the difference between (1) *S* is *F* and (2) *S* is not *F*. It is a difference between the positive and negative acts of the same logical capacity. If we associate this capacity with the *predicate* ". . . is *F*," then the contradictory difference will be *neither* external *nor* internal to the predicative. Not external, since it is associated with the predicate. But not internal, since it is not a predicative difference. (It is a syncategorematic difference.)

I will return to clarify these points in Chapter 2.

4. Language Is Critical

4.1.

A thought is present to the judging subject, says Frege, when it is *grasped*.[44] He calls the process through which we grasp a thought "the most mysterious

---

[43] Capacities *meta logou* are two-way capacities because they involve logical capacities. It is because doctors must *judge* how best to heal their patients that they can also judge how best to poison them.

[44] *Grasping* suggests an achievement, which we may feel tempted to describe as an understanding. We can understand or fail to understand jokes, diagrams, or headlines. To

process." It seems to involve a *sensible* consciousness of the propositional sign. The mystery is how the *logos*—the thought—becomes flesh in the sensible consciousness of a human being.[45] Frege often describes propositional signs in platonistic terms, as the outer *clothing* of a thought. He writes:

> The connection of a thought with one particular proposition is not a necessary one; but that a thought of which we are conscious is connected in our minds with some proposition or other is for us men necessary.
>
> But that does not lie in the nature of thought but in our own nature. There is no contradiction in supposing there to exist beings that can grasp the same thought as we do without needing to clad it in the form that can be perceived by the senses. But still, for us men there is this necessity.[46]

Frege cannot rule out the possibility of nonlinguistic thinkers—or *Fregean intellects,* as I will call them—since he holds that the capacity for intellectual engagement with content—grasping, judging, inferring—is separable from the capacity to express it in language. But it follows from Frege's logical theory that intellectual engagements *with intellectual engagements*— assessing one's inference as valid or recognizing a judgment as a logical truth—are *not* separable from the capacity to express those engagements with content by means of language.

Frege himself says that an assertion "manifests" a judgment (where judging is acknowledging a thought as true).[47] But *manifestation* here splits into two

---

understand such things is to know what they say, or mean. But this cannot be what Frege intends. A Fregean *thought* is not something that *has* content. It *is* a content.

[45] Here is Frege:

> Yes, indeed, but it is a process which takes place on the very confines of the mental and which for that reason cannot be completely understood from a purely psychological standpoint. For in grasping the law something comes into view whose nature is no longer mental in the proper sense, namely the thought; and this process is perhaps the most mysterious of all. ("Logic" [1897], in *Posthumous Writings,* 145)

[46] Frege, "Sources of Knowledge of Mathematics and Natural Sciences," in *Posthumous Writings,* 269.

[47] Cf. "Thought":

> [I]t is possible to express a thought without laying it down as true. The two things are so closely joined in an assertoric sentence that it is easy to overlook their separability. Consequently we distinguish:

different notions: (i) an outer expression of an inner actuality; and (ii) a presentation of a content of a judgment by the composition of a propositional sign in such a way that renders apparent its relations to other contents. Let us call the first *expressive* manifestation and the second *logical* manifestation.

Frege takes the *manifestation* of judgment by assertion to be a composite of expressive and logical manifestation. The inner functionalist composition of a proposition sign manifests the logical identity of a judgment, whereas the assertoric form of the sign expressively manifests the actuality of a judgment that possesses the logical identity in question. The expressive manifestation gives a symbolic presence to the subjective dimension of the act that lies outside the content. This role makes the syncategorematic assertoric form an essentially linguistic device.

The assertoric form in the guise of the vertical judgment stoke is essential for the specification of principles of inference. The acceptance of such principles of inference cannot be identified with a judgment. Rather, such principles must be understood as encapsulating an essentially linguistic capacity that comes with the acquisition and mastery of the *Begriffsschrift*. The capacity is for recognizing the logical relations between contents—one that underwrites one's right to hold something on the basis of other things that one holds. It is a *linguistic* one: for the recognition of these relations essentially depends on our capacity to recognize relations in the graphical form of propositional signs that structurally manifest the content of our acts. Hence, for Frege, the consciousness of our thinking as valid is not separable from the capacity to express our judgments through the use of propositional signs.

In using the judgment stroke, I draw on my capacity to assess my entitlement to a given assertion—where this capacity, in turn, is part and parcel of my overall capacity to employ the notation of the *Begriffsschrift*. In so doing, I thereby understand each of my assertions within the larger normative context of inference within which they have their logical life.

This is why, in the end, it is correct to claim that, for Frege, it is only through the use of language, and particularly through the employment of the assertoric form, that one is able to engage with one's engagement with content. The transition from the judgment "*p*" to the self-consciousness of "I think *p*" can be identified within Frege's system with the transition from

---

(1) the grasp of thought—thinking;

(2) the acknowledgement of the truth of a thought—the act of judgment;

(3) the manifestation of this judgment—assertion. (*The Frege Reader*, 329)

a judgment to the expression of a judgment by an assertion. The judgment-stroke is analogous to "I think."

The idea that we here find in Frege can be called the *linguistic turn* in philosophy.[48]

But since, for Frege—as, for example, the invocation of the possibility of a Fregean intellect shows—the capacity for engagement with content is supposed to be separable from the capacity for language, the linguistic turn as it is taken by Frege is ultimately only partial or incomplete.

That is also why above I described Fregean intellects as being engaged with content, but not with the engagement with content. They are intellectually active but not conscious *of* their intellectual activity. Though they are supposed to be pure intellects, they are not Aristotelian divine intelligences: they cannot think *thinking*. The concept of a Fregean intellect rests on a notion of activity that Kant finds incoherent: a form of intellectual activity separate from self-consciousness of the activity.

By contrast, psycho / logical monism brings with it a *complete* or *full* linguistic turn. In this form of monism, the critical insight—that any unity in consciousness is essentially self-consciousness of that unity—is recognized to coincide with the insight that the consciousness of logical activity is inseparable from the capacity to manifest this activity in language. The complete linguistic turn is the result both of the full context principle that renders Fregean principles of inference superfluous, and the related insight that the repeatability of propositional signs is constitutive of the unity of a contradictory pair and of other logical unities. In other words, the complete linguistic turn lies in a hermeneutic circle: the propositional sign *p* must be comprehended as negatable, and therefore by reference to the logical unity

---

[48] This description is usually used in the literature to name a turn in twentieth-century philosophy toward a concern with language, conceived as a special theme or subject matter, the study of which comes to be regarded as central to making progress with more general and traditional philosophical concerns. This is not how I shall use this term. On the contrary, the expression "linguistic turn" here refers to the idea that the being of thinkers, and thus of human beings, is that of language users, and that the philosophical concern with language is the same as the philosophical concern with thinking and being—moreover, it is the idea that this concern is internal to the use of language. This concern involves a struggle against confusions concerning thinking and being which are created by the "mere look" of signs, a struggle that aims at attaining a clarity that allows signs to do the work of displaying their logical identity for us, the speakers.

of the larger whole which consists in the assertions p, $-p$; this unity of the whole, in turn, depends on the repeatability of the propositional sign p. The point can be generalized to all logical unities.

Monism abolishes the dualist distinction between expressive and logical manifestations through propositional signs in favor of a way of looking at propositional signs in which the logical form itself is, in a sense, expressive.

This way of looking at propositions was outlined in this chapter. We came to see a propositional sign as displaying, by its syncategorematic form, a way of explicating one's activity of thinking.

The generality that is in play in such an explication of consciousness is associated with the syncategorematic form and thus with a propositional sign and not with the generality of a concept. In other words, such an explication is not a determination of consciousness through a predicate.

For example, what is displayed by the propositional sign not-p is an explication of my consciousness as disagreeing with p. The assertion not-p is not an overt proxy for a negative act or negative content in consciousness. Instead, we can say that it explicates the unity of one's consciousness as a whole—a totality—as disagreeing with the assertion p. The assertion not-p is a self-identifying display of a reflective act that is the result of the application of the negation sign to the assertoric gesture p. Thus, the judgment not-p is the same as the assertion not-p—in activity or in spontaneous capacity.

Consider now the positive judgment: the act of judging p is internally related to the use of the propositional sign p in not-p. Hence, the consciousness of the judgment p must be the expression of *it*—in activity or in spontaneous capacity—by the assertion p.

We can conclude that the logical identity of consciousness is displayed through the syncategorematic form of the propositional sign that assertorically manifests it. This cannot be a matter of identifying, depicting or mirroring a bit of actuality in the mind through the composition of a propositional sign. In other words, the propositional sign displays the logical identity of one's thinking as a whole, as a unity, without necessarily depicting or mirroring a component of this unity.

From this point of view, we can see propositional signs with different syncategorematic compositions as displaying one act. In other words, differences in the syncategorematic form of a proposition may come to *nothing*—that is, they have no logical significance. This means that the monist account of propositional complexity is not spatio-logical. For example, the monist, but not the Fregean, can admit that both p and $\sim\sim p$ display the same judgment.[49]

The full or complete linguistic turn liberates us from a picture of thinking or judging as consisting in inner linguistic episodes, i.e., a language-like actuality in the soul, to which the partial linguistic turn seems to be committed.[50]

We can come to recognize now that what distinguishes language from non-linguistic systems of communication or representation—the essence of language—lies in the unity and difference of non-representational, syncategorematic, expressions (e.g., "I," "not . . .") and the representational categorematic expressions that together compose complex linguistic expressions.

4.2.

Once we get rid of the spatio-logical picture and adopt a point of view that acknowledges the full context principle, we can see the repetition of propositional signs within certain propositional contexts as tautologies—namely, as self-cancelling propositional displays. For example, no assertion is displayed by the repetition of the assertoric gesture p within the context of the operation: (. . . & not___). I use the term tautology here generically, so as to refer both to what we can call tautology in the specific sense (p and not-p), as well as contradiction (p and not-p). As such, both tautologies (in the specific sense) and contradictions are tautologies in the sense of self-cancelling displays. Without giving a rigorous definition or characterization of the difference we can say that contradiction is self-canceled as (p and not-p), whereas tautology is self-canceled as (p or not-p).

This notion of tautology as self-cancelling is a by-product of the full context principle. Thus, the self-cancelling application of the operation sign (. . . & ___) to the assertoric gestures "p" and "not-p," reveals the logical unity of contradictory acts. It is in this sense that the full linguistic turn allows us to recognize that the limit one wishes to demarcate by the principle

---

[49] It can also be shown that the monist, but not the Fregean, can see the proposition "a is bigger than b" as only formally different from "b is smaller than a."

[50] As the medium of self-conscious activity, language must include categorematic and syncategorematic expressions. But what distinguishes language from nonlinguistic forms of representation lies in the syncategorematic words ("I," "not . . . ," etc.). These correspond to nonpredicative transitions from consciousness to self-consciousness. (Of course, a language must have other words too—including those that occur in simple predicative propositions.)

of noncontradiction is in fact a limit that is internal to the propositional signs that display judgments. This conception of the limit expressed by the principle of non-contradiction does not succumb to the illusion that the principle demarcates the thinkable by specifying something unthinkable.

4.3.

From the monist point of view

(1) p and not-p

is self-cancelling as contradictory and therefore, given Wittgenstein's point, so is

(2) A thinks (p and not-p).

Moreover, from this point of view, A itself is an "I" and therefore there cannot be a logical gap between (a) A thinks p and A thinks q and (b) A thinks (p and q). Consequently, since (2) is self-cancelling, so too is (3) A thinks p and A thinks not-p. Thus, given Wittgenstein's point we can recognize the sameness of the logical and psychological principles of non-contradiction. This point can be glossed as follows: by thinking 'A thinks p' one is entering into a possible agreement or disagreement with A concerning p, according to whether or not one also thinks p. Hence, "A thinks p" is incompossible with "A thinks not-p." We can see that the self-cancelling contradictoriness of (3) rests on (1); however, their logical unity is not one of simple instantiation (i.e., (3) is not merely an instantiation of (1)), pace the standard reading of Aristotle.

Thus (1) and (3) differ only syncategorematically. Since the negation of (1) is an expression of OPNC and the negation of (3) is an expression of PPNC, these also differ syncategorematically. We can say: they are neither one principle nor two.

The pair <A thinks p, A thinks not-p>, by contrast to <p, not-p> consists of what we can call logical contraries, rather than the members of a contradictory pair, since

(4) A thinks p or A thinks not-p

can be false (A may have no opinion as to whether p).

CHAPTER TWO

The Dominant Sense of Being

1. *Kuriôtata*

Readers of Aristotle have long been perplexed by *Metaphysics* Theta 10—both because of what it says about its topic and because it seems out of place in the context of Theta, as well as the development of the *Metaphysics* as a whole.

Theta 1–9 is devoted to the investigation of the concepts of *dunamis* ("capacity" or "potentiality") and *energeia* ("activity" or "actuality") and to the senses of "being" that are correlated with them. Theta 10, which concludes the book, starts by recapitulating the three senses of being—arguably in the order in which they are presented in the *Metaphysics:* first, the senses of being that correspond to figures of predication—that is, to the categories—which are discussed before Theta; second, being as activity and capacity, which are discussed in the first nine chapters of Theta; and third, being as being-true and non-being as being-false, the topic to which chapter 10 is devoted.

The opening passage of Theta 10[1] already raises the following puzzles concerning the chapter itself:

---

[1] "Since being and not being are said on the one hand in accordance with the figures of the categories and on the other in accordance with the potentiality or actuality of these or of their opposites, and third as what is in the most proper way true or false, and since this as regards things is as the result of their being combined or divided, so that that person speaks the truth who thinks what is divided to be divided, and what is combined to be combined, and the person whose thinking is in the opposite way to the things speaks falsely—when is there or is there not what is termed truth or falsity? For

1. The puzzle raised by the chapter's place within the *Metaphysics* as a whole: The fourfold division of senses of being in Epsilon 4 includes, in addition to the three senses which appear in Theta 10, being in the sense of accidental being. Aristotle goes on in Epsilon 4 to put aside both being in the sense of accidental being, and being in the sense of being-true, as irrelevant to the investigation of being. Being in the sense of being-true is irrelevant, he states, because it does not belong to things but to thought *(dianoia)*. Thus, in Theta 10 Aristotle focuses on a topic that he had previously set aside as irrelevant, and apparently contradicts himself by maintaining that being in the sense of being-true belongs to things.

2. The puzzle raised by the chapter's place within Book Theta: this discussion is placed as the concluding chapter of a book devoted to the seemingly unrelated topic of capacity and activity and the correlated senses of being, i.e., being in the sense of being-in-capacity and being-in-activity.

3. The puzzle raised by the superlative: Aristotle describes being in the sense of being-true and non-being in the sense of being-false by the adverb *kuriôtata* (1051b1), meaning proper, dominant, or governing, and—apparently contradicting Eta 4—he states that being-true exists in things.

The term *kuriôtata* suggests that there is a hierarchy among the senses of being, but the commentators fail to find such a conception in Aristotle.

Some have been led by these problems to exclude chapter 10 from Theta all together; for example, Martin Heidegger reports that Albert Schwegler excluded it on the grounds that the problem of truth belongs to logic, while Theta is principally concerned with fundamental issues in metaphysics. And Werner Jaeger considered Theta 10 to be an appendix which Aristotle added after the rest of the book was completed. For Jaeger, the more serious problem was that being-true should be called *kuriôtata,* viz., the most proper or governing sense of being. "To me," he writes,

> this is very improbable, and it will strike everyone else likewise. If anyone were to support the placement of Θ10 on the ground that only here is the κυριώτατα ὄν attained, he would misunderstand the wording, and besides, he would be thinking in an un-Aristotelian way. (Jaeger, *Studien*

---

it has to be considered what we mean by this. For it is not because of our truly thinking you to be pale that you are pale, but it is rather because you are pale that we who say this speak the truth" (1051a34ff.).

Zur Entwicklungsgeschichte [Berlin 1912], 52; quoted in Heidegger, *The Essence of Freedom: An Introduction to Philosophy,* trans. Ted Sadler [New York: Continuum, 2002], 57–58)

A number of commentators have simply ignored the occurrence of the problematic *kuriôtata;* a few have, with Ross, excised it from the text. Jaeger's own solution was to take it to denote the "prevalent" use—which, however, Heidegger rules out on the grounds that the claim would then be *false:* for being-true is not the most common sense of being.

Jaeger's strong polemic prompted a rebuke from Heidegger, who in *The Essence of Human Freedom* inverts the polemical statements:

> Jaeger wants to say that whoever maintains that Aristotle in Θ10 conceives being-true as the most proper being does not understand what kuriôtata means, moreover has a concept of being quite foreign to Aristotle.
>
> I maintain, by contrast, that anyone who conceives of Θ10 as belonging to Θ, and sees it as the genuine culmination of Θ and of Aristotle's *Metaphysics* as such, thinks not just in properly Aristotelian terms, but simply in Greek terms. The fact that Aristotle closes with Θ10, interpreting being-true as proper being, *indicates that Greek metaphysics' fundamental conception of being here comes to its first and ultimate radical expression.* Only someone who uncritically accepts long-standing traditional platitudes about Aristotle could regard this as un-Aristotelian.

Later he adds:

> *In Θ10 there is concentrated the most radical conception of the basic problem of* Θ. In a word: Θ10 is not a foreign appendix, but rather *the keystone of Book* Θ, which itself is the center of the entire *Metaphysics.* (73–74)

One can find a similar assessment of the significance of Theta 10 in Charles Kahn's work on the verb *to be* in Greek philosophy. It was widely assumed that, by successfully disambiguating the copula "is," through a distinction between existential, predicative, and is-of-identity uses, modern philosophy (i.e., the works of J. S. Mill, Frege, and Russell) had thrown light on the use of the verb *esti (. . . is)* or *einai (to be)* in philosophical contexts— either by pointing to conflations that underpin the ancient discussions, or alternatively by showing that these discussions are already sensitive to such distinctions.

In a series of influential papers, Kahn argues that the coherent unity of the uses of the copula in ancient philosophical works eludes those who try to dissect it through an analytical disambiguation of this kind. Kahn downplays the significance of the so-called existential "is" in Greek philosophy, and insists on the centrality of two other uses of *esti,* the copulative or predicative use, along with the less familiar *veridical* use, which is the use of "is" in ". . . is true" or ". . . is the case."

Kahn notices that there is a split within the veridical use itself:

> "To be true" is not quite the same thing as "to be the case." What is true or false is normally a statement made in words; what is the case or not the case is a fact or situation in the world. The veridical use of *einai* may mean either one (or both), just as our own idiom "it is so" may refer either to a statement or to the fact stated. Now there is a one-to-one correspondence between what is the case and the truth of the statement that it is the case. The statement that the door is open is true if and only if the door is in fact open. Of this necessary connection between truth and fact, no confusion normally results from the ambiguity in the veridical use of *einai.* ("The Greek Verb 'to Be,' and the Concept of Being," 25)

Thus he maintains that the coherence of the prephilosophical veridical use of "is" depends on the assumption of a correspondence or correlation between two kinds of veridical being: on the one hand, what is said and thought (judgments/assertions), and on the other, what is the case or the way things are (facts).

Philosophy emerged in ancient Greek, according to Kahn, from the foregrounding of this prephilosophical veridical use of the complete copula (a copula not explicitly complemented by a predicate). He writes:

> My claim, then, is that in the formation of the Greek concept of Being, the key notion is that of truth—the goal of science and the proper aim of declarative speech. If we bear in mind the structure of the veridical use of the verb, we will easily see how the philosophers' interest in knowledge and truth, taken together with this use of "to be," immediately leads to the concept of Being as reality. I repeat, I am using "reality" here not in any large metaphysical

sense but simply as a convenient term for the facts that make true statements true and false statements false, or for whatever it is "in the world," for whatever "is the case," that makes some assertions and some judgments correct and others mistaken. If I assert—either in thought or in speech—that the sun is shining, and if what I assert is true, then the corresponding "reality" is simply the fact that the sun is shining. ("Existence is not a Distinct Concept in Greek," in *Essays on Being*, 68–69)

Like Heidegger, Kahn sees Theta 10 as an outstanding manifestation of "the Greek concept of being":

These remarks are intended to render plausible my claim that, for the philosophical usage of the verb, the most fundamental value of *einai* when used alone (without predicates) is not "to exist" but "to be so," "to be the case," or "to be true." It is worth noting that this meaning of the verb, which appears among the four uses listed in the chapter of *Met.* Δ summarized above (where Aristotle recognizes the sense of truth even in the predicative construction, when *esti* appears in the emphatic initial position, 1017 a 33–5), is elsewhere described by Aristotle as the "strictest" or "most authoritative" sense of "to be" (*Met.* Θ 10. 1051 b 1: *to kuriôtata on*). Recent editors, notably Ross and Jaeger, are unhappy about this statement, and would like to "emend" it in various ways. My argument suggests that they are wrong, and that the text is entirely in order. I understand Aristotle to be saying that, from a philosophic point of view, this use of *einai* is the most basic and the most literal meaning of the verb. ("The Greek Verb 'to Be,' and the Concept of Being," 23)

There are serious weaknesses in Kahn's account of the veridical use which arise from his assumption that the intrinsic being—the existence—of a veridical being is separate from its veridical being, which is expressed by the use of the veridical verb. Firstly, he is committed to the idea that the coherence of the veridical use depends on a philosophically dubious conception of truth as correspondence (more on this later). Secondly, Kahn wishes to join the consensus among commentators by acknowledging the centrality of the predicative use of the copula in Greek philosophy—but he fails, in the end, to give a convincing account that subsumes the veridical use under the predicative use, even in the case of elementary sentences.

The question concerning the relation between the predicative and veridical senses of *being* is one of the challenging puzzles posed by Theta 10. I propose to address it by scrutinizing carefully the notions of *combination (synthesis)* and *separation (diairesis)* which Aristotle associates, on the one hand, with predicative form, and on the other hand, with the notions of truth and falsity as such. Our aim is to show that the veridical "to be" is, in a way, both existential and predicative. To that end, I will focus on the discussion contained in chapters 4–6 of *De Interpretatione* that leads to the introduction of the notion of contradictory pairs *(antiphasis).*

2. The Revealing *Logos*

The topic of *De Interpretatione* 4 is a certain type of *logos* (i.e., a sentence or statement) which Aristotle calls *apophantic*—for, he says,

> not every *logos* is *apophantic,* but only that in which being true or being false is found. But they are not found in all *logoi:* e.g., prayer is a *logos* but it [is] neither true nor false. (17a1ff.)

Apophantikos is conventionally translated as "assertoric," "declarative," or "statement-making," but this does not convey its full meaning, for the verb *apophanein* literally means "to show" or "to reveal." It thus belongs to a recurring theme of *De Interpretatione.* In the first chapter, for instance, the affections of the soul expressed by *logoi* are described as likenesses *(homoiômata)* of things *(pragmata);* in the fifth chapter the simple *logos apophantikos* is characterized as revealing or showing *(dêlôn)* a single thing *(pragma).*

These motives will be familiar to readers of Wittgenstein's *Tractatus,* with its account of propositions as pictures. There is, I believe, an affinity between these works—a shared, and almost unique, insight into the *logos apophantikos.* I will try to bring this out in what follows.

3. Acts

From the discussion of signification in *De Int.* 1 it transpires that the *logos apophantikos* is a linguistic expression (i.e., a symbol) for an *affection* of the soul. Today we call this sort of affection a *judgment,* meaning a certain type of mental *act.* This use of the term *act* requires careful scrutiny, however.

For a judgment is not the sort of thing one decides to do, an *intentional* action. The scholarly response to this is to point out that "act" is meant in the philosophical sense of an *actuality*, as contrasted with a *potentiality*. This response is unsatisfying, however, since it is clear that in describing judgment as an *act* philosophers have meant to invoke the agency, in *some* sense, of the judging subject. A devoted student will remind us at this point of the Aristotelian notion of actuality, namely, of *energeia* and specifically of Aristotle's notion of an *activity* which contains its end. A judgment, as an *activity* in this sense, is neither a product nor a process, but is instead the very maintaining of one's conscious agreement with oneself concerning something. This understanding of judgment as an activity, in the sense of self-maintenance, is said to capture Kant's notion of judgment as a synthesis, i.e., a combination.

Indeed, this characterization of judgment involves a rejection of the Stoics' or Frege's notion of judgment as assent or dissent to a truth-bearer whose unity is given independently of these acts. But we shall find that the deeper source of dissatisfaction with the use of term *act* for judgment, and of talk of *reason* or *understanding* as powers or capacities of judgment, emerges once we overcome this Stoic / Fregean conception and come to see what follows from the understanding of judgment as subjective *combination / synthesis.*

Our conclusion will be that, where "A" is a proper name of a person (or a definite description of a person), and "ψ's" is an expression such as "doubts," "thinks," "judges," "hopes," or "asserts," a proposition of the form (S1) A ψ's that *p,* is not a predicative determination of a person. In contrast, propositions of the form (S2) This F is φ-ing, where F is a kind of animal, and φ is a verb, are predicative determinations. In general, capacities and acts are possible determinations of a living being and so the deep logical difference between (S1) and (S2) is easy to ignore when we describe thinking or judging in terms of faculties or powers and their activities. (The question which now arises, and which I don't pretend to address directly here, is how to understand a proposition of the form (S3) A is φ-ing. That is, how to understand the sense in which a thinker is a determinable being.)

4. *Synthesis* and *Diairesis*

In *De Int.* 1.1 Aristotle says that "falsity and truth have to do with combination *(synthesis)* and separation *(diairesis)*." The being of what can be true or false must therefore be understood in terms of these notions.

It is widely accepted in the literature that combinations and separations are, for Aristotle, contrasting ways of bringing together subject and predicate terms into a predicative unity. The difference between combination and separation is thus commonly taken to be between two predicative forms: positive and negative. But this, I would argue, is a serious error that cannot be ascribed to Aristotle. Instead, I want to suggest that though combination and separation (as he understands them) do not lie *outside* the predicative form they nonetheless are not internal to the predicative form.

The implication is that *the synthesis* which is immanent to the subject-predicate proposition does not fully lie within the predicative. I hope to convey that I am not advancing some sort of philosophical mysticism that points toward an original unity lying beyond the predicative. (Yet in light of this point, one wonders whether the mystics are looking in the wrong place when they seek the nonpredicative outside of the *logos*.)

5. The List of Propositions

De Int. 1.5 opens with a list of three logical types of proposition *(logos apophantikos)*. The first Aristotle calls "affirmation" *(kataphasis)*; the second he calls "negation" or "denial" *(apophasis);*[2] and the third is that of the various compounds that, he says, are "single by virtue of a connective" (17a8). The list is ordered by priority: affirmation, i.e., a positive predication, is prior to negation, i.e., a negative predication, which in turn is prior to compound propositions. As we shall come to see, this priority does not entail independence. It is not the case that what is prior in this list is independent, either in its being or its intelligibility, from what is posterior in it. I shall argue, for example, that negation is indeed parasitic on affirmation, and yet that affirmation contains within it, in some sense, the contrast to negation. In

[2] In the recent literature "denial" is a term for negative assertoric force, and "negation" is a term for a propositional connective as well as a proposition insofar as it is governed by this connective. Frege, of course, denies that there is any such thing as "denial." It is commonly assumed that Aristotle holds that a predicative negation of the form "*S* is not *F*" displays a negative force, namely, a predicative denial. But I shall argue that this assumption is wrong, that Aristotle agrees with Frege, and that there is no such thing as denial understood as a negative act. Which is nevertheless not to say that for Aristotle negation is, as Frege has it, a content modifier.

other words, affirmation is prior to negation, but the unity of the contradictory pair dominates it.

From the point of view of modern logic the negation sign is a propositional connective, which means that the difference between a subject-predicate proposition and its negation—a difference marked by the negation sign—is one of propositional form, and thus external to the subject-predicate unity. The occurrence of "negation" as a distinct item on Aristotle's list indicates, however, that he does not take it to be a propositional connective—as, for example, Elizabeth Anscombe has claimed. "Aristotle," she says,

> has not the idea of the negation of a proposition, with the negation sign outside the whole proposition—that was (I believe) invented by the Stoics. ("Aristotle and the Sea Battle," in *The Collected Papers of Elizabeth Anscombe, Vol. 1: From Parmenides to Wittgenstein* [Oxford: Basil Blackwell, 1981], 44)

Anscombe seems to conclude that Aristotle's negation works internally within the predicative proposition[3] by modifying the predicative form (i.e., the relation of the predicate to the subject term). C. W. A. Whitaker, who agrees with Anscombe, proposes a piece of notation to clarify Aristotle's notion of affirmation and negation:

> Aristotle . . . sees a negation as an assertion which alleges the separation of elements which an affirmation represents as combined. A better notation to represent this view would be to write the affirmation as "$a + b$" and the negation as "$a < b$": this would reflect Aristotle's belief that negation is internal to the assertion, and involves altering the relation between subject and predicate from combination to separation. (*Aristotle's De Interpretatione: Contradiction and Dialectic* [Oxford: Oxford University Press, 1997], 81)

Whitaker's interpretation identifies affirmation and negation with combination and separation as two ways of relating a subject term and a predicate. Later I will argue that this interpretation of negation is incoherent since it precludes us from seeing that affirmation occurs within negation, namely,

---

[3] In fact, there are two ways that negation can be regarded as propositional or external. For the Stoics, the negation sign indicated negative assertoric force, a dissent from the proposition that has been put forward; for Frege, by contrast, the negation has a different content than the negated proposition, so that the negation sign displays the dependence of the compound content on the negated content.

that "*S* is *F*" occurs within "*S* is not *F*"; for now I just want to note that it is hard to square with Aristotle's list of proposition types. For one thing, it cannot account for the *priority* of affirmation to negation, since it treats them as two kinds of predication, i.e., as two predicative forms on equal footing. For another thing, a negation of a compound cannot be an internal negation, since a compound, according to Aristotle, does not have a predicative form. It is thus utterly unclear how such a notion of predicative negation can be extended to include the negation of compounds.

Does Aristotle therefore recognize two types of negation—one that is internal to simple predications and another that is external to them? Hopefully not, since that will obscure the logical character of propositions like "not-(*p* or *q*) and *p*," which is a contradiction, and of "not-(*p* and *q*) or *q*," which is a tautology.

I will argue, *pace* Anscombe and Whitaker, that Aristotle does not take negation to be internal to the predicative form; and yet it is undeniable that for Aristotle, in contrast, say, to the Stoics and the Fregeans, negation cannot be described as external to the predicative. We can see this if we compare their respective approaches to the principle of noncontradiction (PNC).

From the Fregean point of view, PNC applies to any pair of propositions *p* and not-*p* in virtue of their propositional form, and therefore independently of the internal form of *p,* and so in particular PNC applies to a simple pair of predications in virtue of propositional rather than predicative form.

By contrast, Aristotle's principle of noncontradiction applies primarily to affirmation and negation *precisely in virtue of their predicative form.* Thus, the understanding of the unity of predication coincides with the understanding of the necessity expressed by the principle.

Aristotle's negation, I will propose, is neither external to predicative form, i.e., a propositional connective, nor internal to it as a negative form of predication. (Once this has been established it will become clear that the notion of predicative negation can be extended to encompass a general notion of negation that also applies to compounds.)[4]

---

[4] Frege recognizes, of course, the negation of a predicate in contrast to the negation of a proposition. He notes, however, that in the case of simple propositions it makes no difference whether we attach the negation sign to the predicate or to the proposition as a whole. I will argue that the same holds for Aristotle's account.

6. *De Interpretatione* 5: The Elements of Discourse

The topic of *De Int.* 5 is the elements of discourse and their unities, where an *element of discourse* is not a mere sound but a "significant sound" *(phônê sêmantikê)* which as such is identifiable by its logical use (16b26.) It turns out there are two ways such elements can constitute a propositional unity: (1) as simple propositions, i.e., by affirming or denying something of something; or (2) as compound propositions, i.e., complexes of simple propositions. There are also two ways an element of discourse can signify without constituting a propositional unity: (3) as a component of simple propositions, i.e., a name *(onoma)* or a verb *(rhêma);* or (4) as a manifold of propositions. (Aristotle does not give an example of (4), but presumably he is thinking, among other things, of the propositions held together as premises of a syllogism.)

Among these elements Aristotle singles out simple propositions as *revealing* something. In other words, only simple propositions are representations. They alone *say*—or *display the judgment*—that something is (or is not) the case.[5] They alone reveal a being. Of course, this does not tell us what is meant by "revealing," or what "being" is revealed by the proposition. For now, however, what matters is that this revealing is associated with the predicative force that is displayed by the verb in a simple proposition (i.e., *affirming* or *denying* something of something).

Given the association of *revealing* with predicative force, then, the following question arises: How is the predicative unity revealing, or *sui generis* representational?

Many readers have thought that the answer lies in the iconic role of combination and separation: that what a proposition reveals is a state of affairs, *its truth maker,* which it depicts or mirrors as a combination or separation of elements. For example, Whitaker—who wants to represent affirmation and negation as the pair "$a + b$," "$a − b$"—would also represent the states of affairs revealed by them respectively as "$A + B$" and "$A − B$," where *a* refers to *A,*

---

[5] I will use the formulas "*p says* that *p*" and "*p displays* the judgment that *p*" interchangeably; *p* displays a judgment that *p* if this judgment is expressible by the assertion *p*. I will return to this below.

and *b* to *B*. Briefly, the problem with this proposal is that since "*A* + *B*" is isomorphic to "*A* – *B*" there is nothing about "*a* + *b*" which identifies it as revealing the positive situation "*A* + *B*," rather than the negative "*A* – *B*." This suggests that revealing is not in fact a matter of sharing a common form—of which more below.

Insofar as a compound proposition is governed by a connective that is not a verb, it is not predicative according to Aristotle. It does not reveal that something is (or is not) the case. Accordingly, there are no such things as compound states of affairs—yet the compound proposition certainly has a truth-value. There is, then, this further question too: How can a truth-evaluable unity be attained *in virtue of a connective,* and so by reference to whatever the subordinate propositions reveal?

Philosophers following Frege will of course refuse the question: for them, *all* truth-evaluable propositions are claims that something is the case. Philosophers who use Fregean materials to introduce a deflationary notion of a state of affairs seem to be committed to the notion of compound *facts:* not just "*p* & *q*" but also "*p* or *q*." Moreover, according to this kind of account, the fact that *p* must be different from the fact that not-not-*p*.

7. The Categorematic and the Syncategorematic

I shall propose that Aristotle's claim that the propositional unity attained by a connective does not reveal a single being, i.e., a unity, rests on an interpretation of logical connectives as *syncategorematic* expressions. The notion of the syncategorematic (and the categorematic) which is in play here should be carefully distinguished from a familiar *semantic notion of the syncategorematic* which invokes an intuitive idea of what is and is not referentially significant. I shall first introduce this familiar semantic notion of the syncategorematic in order to put it aside in favor of another notion that I shall call the *literal notion of the syncategorematic,* which will be useful in throwing light on Aristotle's claim concerning compounds.

"Syncategorematic" as a technical term in logic originated in late antiquity and is often introduced in the literature by invoking Aristotle's principle of the copulas "to be" or "not to be" from *De Int.* 3: "by itself it is nothing, but it additionally signifies [cosignifies] some combination, which cannot be thought of without the components" (16b23–25). On this understanding, a syncategorematic expression, or a syncategorematic feature of a proposition, is taken to be one that simply indicates the form of composition of a proposition without being semantically associated with any worldly entity. This semantical notion of the *syncategorematic* presupposes that a proposition is analyzable into a nonreferring compositional nexus and referentially significant (categorematic) components, i.e., into compositional form and semantical matter.

It is often remarked that Frege's functionalist conception of propositional complexity renders this notion of the *syncategorematic* obsolete by associating the propositional nexus in a simple proposition with the predicate, which Frege characterizes as referentially significant. Frege's notion of what it is to be referentially significant, which simply coincides with the notion of being a logical component, cannot be understood in terms of the intuitive sense of "reference" that is based on the paradigm of a name and its bearer. Since the semantic notion of the syncategorematic is based on this intuitive notion, Frege's characterization of a predicate as having a concept as its reference hardly shows that his notion of a predicate is categorematic. As such, the question whether or not Frege's notion of a predicate is syncategorematic is arguably meaningless.[6]

Furthermore, it is also not clear how the characterization of the propositional form as having no significance of its own coheres with the position that is often ascribed to Aristotle (and Wittgenstein), that the form of a proposition depicts the form of the corresponding fact. Why, one could ask, is it that this kind of iconic semantical import, i.e., the depiction of a form, is not semantically or even referentially significant?

---

[6] Frege describes a concept-word as having a *function,* i.e., a concept, as its reference. In the Fregean framework two expressions are said to have the same *reference* (or meaning, *Bedeutung*) when they can be substituted for one another without affecting the truth of the propositions in which they appear. Consequently, anything that allows for substitution in a proposition (or more generally in a complex expression) must be regarded as referential. But it is not hard to show that there cannot be a relational predicate: "reference," in Frege's *Begriffsschrift,* through which the references of names and of predicate expressions are specifiable. In other words, there is no univocal sense of "reference" according to which both names and predicates can be described as referring. Moreover, since Frege describes the predicate as the locus of combination in a simple proposition, he would agree with Aristotle that a predicate only signifies as a nexus of combination within a logical whole.

In any case, the semantic notion of the syncategorematic fails to illuminate Aristotle's claim that the propositional unity effected by connectives is
nonrevealing (of a single being, a unity). After all, many commentators have
ascribed to Aristotle the view that a propositional unity, held together by a
syncategorematic copula, is in fact revealing, and so if both logical connectives and copula are syncategorematic there is no reason why a compound
will not be equally revealing.

But I wish to point to another philosophical use of the terms *categorematic* and *syncategorematic* which is derived directly from the Greek word
katêgoria ("predicate") and is not based on semantic criteria. A *categorematic*
expression or term is one that can significantly occur within a predicative
proposition, while a *syncategorematic* expression is one that cannot play a significant role within a predicative proposition. The basic syncategorematic
expressions, according to this use of the term, will turn out to be predicative propositions—which are indeed the "syn" of categorematic expressions.
We shall see later that this literal notion of the syncategorematic—which
exploits the literal meaning of "syn"—captures some of the intuitions concerning the distinction between merely formal and referentially significant
expressions that the semantical notion of the syncategorematic is trying to
convey. From now on I shall use the terms syncategorematic and categorematic according to this literal notion.

It is clear that according to the formal understanding of the categorematic-
syncategorematic distinction, in simple propositions the subject and predicate terms and even the copula (if one wishes to identify it as the propositional nexus distinct from the predicate term) are categorematic. Among the
candidates for being classed as syncategorematic are logical connectives
such as . . . *and*__, and . . . *or*__, expressions of propositional attitudes such
as . . . *believes*__, and truth-value predicates such as . . . *is true* and . . . *is
false*. We can describe these expressions as *propositional connectors,* since they
govern propositions that have other propositions as their subclauses. The
question whether these connectors are syncategorematic expressions raises
the further, more fundamental, question whether simple predicative propositions themselves are categorematic or syncategorematic units.

A predicative proposition is a categorematic *unit* if something can be
predicated of it, or if it can be predicated of something—in other words,
if it can stand as a subject or a predicate in a proposition. A proposition is
a syncategorematic unit if it cannot play a categorematic role, namely, if

it cannot occur within a predicative proposition. If simple propositions are syncategorematic units, then the larger propositional contexts in which they occur must be governed by syncategorematic connectors. Hence, the *logical connective* ". . . and___," the *indirect speech/thought connector* "A says . . ." / "A believes . . . ," and the *truth connector* ". . . is true" are all syncategorematic.

Whereas according to the semantical notion of the syncategorematic the *syn* purports to pick out the formal element in a proposition which is the *nexus* of combination, according to the literal notion of the syncategorematic the *syn* points to the simple proposition as a whole and thus to the nonpredicative contexts in which the whole proposition can occur.

The distinction Aristotle draws in *De Int.* 5 between the unity of simple propositions and the unity of compound propositions implies that a compound proposition is not predicative. I shall argue later that Aristotle's characterization of a contradictory pair of simple predications as *combination* and *separation* implies that a simple proposition is a syncategorematic unit, and therefore that negation and logical connectives are syncategorematic expressions.

By contrast, for Frege propositions are categorematic units and all expressions are univocally categorematic. This difference between Aristotle and Frege is rooted in their different understanding of predicative form itself.

For Aristotle, the predicative form displays the assertoric act of predication, which he associates with the verb. Accordingly, in traditional Aristotelian logic, the verb (i.e., the predicate) in a simple proposition is marked as the locus of predication and thus the locus of assertoric force.

In his short posthumous piece "A Brief Survey of My Logical Doctrines," Frege placed the following at the top of his list:

Dissociating the assertoric force from the predicate.[7]

---

[7] The term "dissociating" suggests that Frege's claim is stronger than the mere denial that the predicate actually contains, i.e., expresses, assertoric force. The difference between the weaker and stronger claims turns out to be crucial to gaining a correct understanding of the predicate.

Geach hails Frege for attaining an epochal victory over ancient philosophical folly with his dissociation of force from the predicate:

> It took the genius of the young Frege to dissolve the monstrous and unholy union that previous logicians had made between the import of the predicate and the assertoric force of a proposition. Even when a proposition has assertoric force, this attaches to the proposition as a whole, not specially to the subject, or to the predicate, or to any part of a proposition.[8]

The characterization of assertoric force here as being attached to "the proposition as a whole" is misleading as a formulation of Frege's position since it suggests that, for example, an assertoric force belongs to the proposition in the way that its truth-value does. The truth-value is external to the logical identity of the proposition which is associated with its content; however, identity in contents secures identity in truth-value. Frege noticed that while logical identity, i.e., content (and therefore truth-value), belongs to a proposition *qua* repeatable, actual force belongs only to particular occurrences of the proposition (Frege's observation). He concluded that no logically significant feature of propositions is associated with assertoric force, and that in particular the predicative unity of a proposition does not contain force (Frege's point). The Fregean doctrine, which became orthodoxy, is that the predicative complexity which is a functional complexity characterizes the judgment only *qua* its content and not *qua* act; *qua* act all judgments are the same. In particular, a compound judgment, on this doctrine, is the same *qua* act as a predicative judgment. By contrast, we can conclude from Aristotle's remark in *De Int.* 5 that simple and compound propositions are different *qua* acts (a formulation which will be qualified later).

By dissociating *assertoric force* from the *predicate,* Frege lost the traditional resource for distinguishing name and predicate (verb) by their roles in simple propositions; yet Frege took it to be the case that his functionalist construal of logical complexity was in fact able to disclose the nature of this difference, which had hitherto been hidden from the tradition. This difference, according Frege, is the difference between the *functional types* that the

---

[8] Peter Geach, *Reference and Generality* (Ithaca, NY: Cornell University Press, 1980), 51.

expressions for the subject and the predicate belong to. Frege held that in a logical notation capable of manifesting the logical dependence of an instance upon a generalization, all propositional signs must be functionally composed by an application of a functional expression to an argument(s) expression(s) of the right level, to use Frege's idiom. The difference between a singular term (name) and a predicate, according to Frege, is the difference between a first-level functional expression of a special kind (i.e., a concept-expression) and the expressions that fill the argument place in a first-level functional expression. To indicate that the functional expressions carry the argument place, Frege describes them as *incomplete* or *unsaturated;*[9] by contrast he describes the argument expressions for a first-level functional expression as complete or saturated. Frege calls such complete expressions *names,* and proposes that ordinary names are complete expressions. Frege glosses the functional difference between name and predicate as a difference between incomplete and complete expressions, and holds that since traditional syllogistic logic could not account for the validity of the inference from a general proposition to

---

[9] Frank Ramsey challenged Frege's view that unsaturatedness is the mark of the predicate in simple propositions by asking the Fregean to explain why a pair of propositions such as (a) *Theaetetus flies* and (b) *Theaetetus sits* are not seen as different saturations of the following incomplete expression: Theaetetus ___.

The context principle implies that a name only has meaning in its logical employment in a proposition, which raises the question why a proposition as a whole is more intimately related to the predicate rather than to the name.

Geach tries to respond to this challenge by invoking an observation Aristotle makes in the *Categories* and that is available within the Fregean framework:

> When a proposition is negated, the negation may be taken as going with the predicate in a way in which it cannot be taken to go with the subject. For predicables always occur in contradictory pairs; and by attaching such a pair to a common subject we get a contradictory pair of propositions. But we never have a contradictory pair of names so related that by attaching the same predicate to both we always get a pair of contradictory propositions. (*Reference and Generality*, 32)

In the same vein, Geach adds that attaching negation to a predicate yields another predicate, but attaching negation to a name does not yield another name. But one can press the question further and ask: Why is negation so intimately associated with the predicate but not with the name? The tradition has a ready answer: the predicate is associated with assertoric force, and so is negation, and consequently they are associated with one another. But this answer is not available to Frege, who regards the dissociation of assertoric force from the predicate, as well as from negation, as his crowning achievement.

an instance, a correct understanding of the difference of name and predicate eluded it.[10] It is a consequence of Frege's functionalist construal of logical complexity that all complete expressions are names, i.e., possible argument expressions in first-level functions. In particular, simple propositions
which are completed first-level functions are *categorematic units* as argument-
expressions for concept expressions, i.e., for predicates. Frege's functionalist
construal of logical complexity leaves no place for anything syncategorematic
in the literal sense.

Thus, for Frege, logical connectives are relational predicates, namely,
concept-expressions, and so, for example, the proposition *p* occurs as one of
the relata in *if p then q,* which is a completion of the functional expression
if . . . then __. Similarly, the truth connector *. . . is true* is a predicate of the
same logical / syntactical category as a monadic logical connective such as
negation, and the connectors of thought / indirect speech: *. . . says___ / . . .
believes __,* are also construed as relational predicates. Logical considerations
force Frege to distinguish logical connectors which are extensional predicates from connectors of ascriptions which are intensional predicates. Two
argument expressions which are extensionally the same are substitutable *salve
veritate* within an extensional predicate but not within an intensional predicate, and thus Frege takes logical connectors to be extensional predicates and
the connectors of ascriptions to be intensional predicates. We shall see soon
that the distinction between the extensional and intensional logical contexts
dissolves when the connectors are interpreted as syncategorematic.

---

[10] But in fact, as we observed in Chapter 1, the functionalist treatment of logical complexity leaves Frege's *Begriffsschrift* without any resources to mark predicates (i.e.,
concept-words) as distinct first-order functional expressions. Hence, the irony in the
very title of the *Begriffsschrift,* since this logical notation fails precisely to mark the
logical character of concept-words *(Begriffswörter),* that is, to symbolize the distinctive
character of unsaturated expressions as having concepts for their reference. The notation cannot mark the difference between a function expression such as *the capital of . . .*
or *2 + . . .* and a concept word such as *. . . is wise.*
   The mark of concept-words that distinguishes them from other first-level functions
is that they are negatable. I would therefore argue that at the fundamental level the
Begriffsschrift fails to distinguish between negatable and nonnegatable functional expressions. Frege's attempt to patch the hole with the *ad hoc* supplement of the content-
stroke, i.e., the horizontal, as some sort of truth-predicate to which logical connectives
are attached, leads to an incoherent decomposition of marked concept-expressions into
parts that signify, and parts that display force.

8. The Unity of a Compound

How can the propositional unity which is attained *in virtue of a connective*
be truth-evaluable by reference to whatever the subordinate propositions reveal without itself revealing a single thing, that is, without representing a
state of affairs as obtaining? We can see this as an instance of the general
question concerning the logical context governed by propositional connectors that are understood as syncategorematic. I propose that to understand
a connector as syncategorematic is to understand it as the sign for an operation in the sense that we introduced in the previous chapter. Let me therefore recall the discussion of logical connectives as *operations,* and more
specifically as *truth/falsity operations.*

A *truth/falsity operation* is a way of identifying one's own consciousness
in terms of agreement and disagreement with certain simple judgments. For
example, if *conjunction* (. . . & __) is a truth operation, then in judging that
p & q, I identify my consciousness as containing the judgments displayed
by the two propositions p and q.

It follows that a compound judgment is merely a spontaneous self-
clarification of consciousness. The (. . . & __) simply displays an action of
self-clarification of consciousness, or self-consciousness. And since this act
is not a categorematic addition to consciousness, or a determination of anything, the transition to self-consciousness can be described as a syncategorematic transition.

9. *De Interpretatione* 6: The Directions of Assertions

De Int. 6 begins by narrowing the topic to simple propositions, i.e., those
that claim that something is or is not the case. These are, respectively, *affirmations (kataphaseis)* and *denials (apophaseis).*[11]

---

[11] Aristotle classifies simple propositions as either singular or categorical. By contrast,
Frege—in the framework of a quantificational analysis of generality—permits only
singular propositions.

But Frege's contribution can be seen as a change of subject rather than as progress,
since (1) Fregean generality, i.e., generality of concepts, cannot capture Aristotelian generality, which is the normative generality of kinds; and (2) Fregean particularity, i.e.,

What these consist in is characterized in two ways. An affirmation, Aristotle says, is "a proposition asserting something *toward* something [*kata tinos*]"; a denial is "a proposition asserting something *away from* something [*apo tinos*]" (17a25). The difference between affirmation and denial is thus a difference in the *direction* of assertion.[12]

How should we understand this?[13] It is worth noting an asymmetry between "pointing toward" and "pointing away from" something. For in the first case the direction of pointing is at least comparatively determinate (as a point in space), while in the second it is not. (We shall see how this asymmetry helps to illuminate the priority of affirmation over negation.)

Elsewhere, however, Aristotle characterizes simple affirmation *(kataphasis)* as "combination" *(synthesis)* and simple negation *(apophasis)* as "separation" *(diairesis)*. The question arises, then, whether a combination is an assertion toward and a separation an assertion away from; or whether the two characterizations in some way diverge.

One place where the characterizations seem to diverge is *De Anima* 3.6, where Aristotle is discussing the notions of combination and separation. He says there that whatever can be false must involve combination and so "even when you assert that what is [in fact] white is not white you have combined non-white. It is also possible to call all these cases separation" (430b1). This passage should give pause to those who understand combination and

---

the particularity of objects, cannot capture Aristotelian particularity, which is the particularity of substances and of tensed propositions.

From Frege's functionalist point of view Aristotle simply failed to see that his categorical propositions are not a kind of simple, i.e., predicative proposition, and that therefore his syllogistic is an incomplete fragment of what can be fully expressed by the quantifier notation of the concept-script. But I would argue that Frege is blinded by his functionalist conception to the possibility of a nonfunctionalist (factualist) understanding of the variables, i.e., of a kind of generality which is compatible with Aristotelian generality and particularity.

[12] Heidegger emphasizes this point:

> That which points out is either a pointing out that *points toward* or a pointing out that *points away*. The board is black, the board is not red. The pointing out can be such as to *ascribe* something to whatever the pointing out is concerned with, or such as to deny it something in pointing it out, i.e., to point something *away* from it: the board is not red. (*The Fundamental Concepts of Metaphysics,* trans. William McNeil and Nicholas Walker [Indianapolis: Indiana University Press, 1983], 316)

[13] See also *Nichomachean Ethics* VI.2: "What affirmation and negation are in thinking, pursuit and avoidance are in desire."

separation as two different ways of relating propositional components. As Heidegger puts it:

> Every *kataphasis*-assertion [i.e., affirmation] is in itself *synthesis* and *diairesis,* likewise every *apophasis,* and it is not as though *kataphasis* is a *synthesis* and *apophasis* a *diairesis.* These distinctions lie in quite different dimensions. Furthermore, the distinction between *synthesis* and *diairesis* is not of the same order as *apophansis,* but rather a distinction that precisely articulates the originary and unitary essence of a structure or a structured phenomenon [namely, of simple predications]. . . .
>
> . . . Being true or false, and thus the entire structure of the *logos apophantikos,* is grounded in *synthesis,* which in itself is simultaneously *diairesis.* (*The Fundamental Concepts of Metaphysics,* 317)

This claim about the unity of combination and separation is puzzling. If combination *(synthesis)* is simultaneously separation *(diairesis),* how should we understand Aristotle's suggestion that positive and negative predication be distinguished as combination and separation—and, moreover, how can we understand it in a way that illuminates the priority of affirmation to negation? The answer, we shall see, lies in Wittgenstein's point. To describe the notions of combination and separation in a way that accords with Wittgenstein's point we shall have to conclude that combination occurs in separation—and that nothing else besides combination does. Moreover, combination must be understood as, essentially, that which can occur in separation.

10. Three Views of the Place of the Semantic in Logic

In trying to make sense of Aristotle's use of the semantic term *revealing* it may be helpful to reflect briefly on the role of the semantical in Aristotle's logical work. Consider again *De Int.* 5, where Aristotle distinguishes two ways of being a single proposition and two ways of being a plurality of propositions:

> A single proposition is either one that reveals *(dêlôn)* a single thing or one that is single in virtue of a connective. There are more than one if more things than one are revealed or if connectives are lacking. (17a15–16)

Recent commentators have complained that Aristotle runs together two different criteria for the singleness of propositions: a semantic criterion that is concerned with the identity of the content, and a syntactic criterion that concerns the form of the propositional sign. For example, Whitaker writes:

> [T]wo different criteria are given for what makes an assertion single (17a15–24). . . . The first criterion is to do with whether the assertion expresses a single claim about a single subject; according to this criterion, an assertion which expresses a multiple sense is really more than one assertion, regardless of its apparent form. This might be called the semantic criterion.
>
> The second criterion is syntactic rather than semantic: according to this, two assertions which have been combined may be considered one by conjunction, while separate assertions which are not conjoined would count as more than one. Applying the two criteria clearly gives a different result. Two assertions linked by "and" would still count as more than one by the semantic criterion, since two distinct claims would be made, but on the syntactic criterion would count as conjoined into a single assertion. We are thus, in effect, given two senses in which an assertion may be said to be single: we are told that a single assertion either reveals one thing or is one by conjunction, and more than one assertion either makes more than one claim or else is not conjoined (17a15–17). (*Aristotle's De Interpretatione*, 75)

The fact that Whitaker finds *syntactical* and *semantical* criteria in Aristotle shows that he reads him through the prism of the modern *schematic conception* of logic, which Warren Goldfarb characterizes as follows:

> [T]he subject matter of logic consists of logical properties of sentences and logical relations among sentences. Sentences have such properties and bear such relations to each other by dint of their having the logical forms they do. Hence, logical properties and relations are defined by way of the logical forms; logic deals with what is common to and can be abstracted from different sentences. Logical forms are not mysterious quasi-entities, à la Russell. Rather, they are simply schemata: representations of the composition of the sentences, constructed from the logical signs (quantifiers and truth-functional connectives, in the standard case) using schematic letters of various sorts (predicate, sentence, and function letters). Schemata do not state anything and so are neither true nor false, but they can be interpreted: a universe of discourse is assigned to the quantifiers, predicate letters are replaced by predicates or assigned extensions (of the appropriate r-ities) over the universe, sentence letters can be replaced by sentences or assigned truth-values. Under interpretation, a schema will receive truth-value. We may then define: a schema is *valid* if and only if it is true under every interpretation; one schema *implies* another, that is, the second schema is a *logical consequence* of the first, if and

only if every interpretation that makes the first true also makes the second true. A more general notion of logical consequence, between sets of schemata and a schema, may be defined similarly. Finally, we may arrive at the logical properties or relations between sentences thus: a sentence is logically true if and only if it can be schematized by a schema that is valid; one sentence implies another if they can be schematized by schemata the first of which implies the second. ("Frege's Conception of Logic," in Thomas Ricketts and Michael Potter, eds., *The Cambridge Companion to Frege* [Cambridge: Cambridge University Press, 2010], 64–65)

Thus, a metalinguistic truth predicate is employed, according to this conception, in defining sentences of the object language as "logical truths" and in characterizing sequences of sentences as "sound" or "valid" arguments. Such metalinguistic characterizations apply to a formal language, namely, to strings that are syntactically identifiable as sentences, and which are generated from a vocabulary of uninterpreted, syntactically marked strings and logical constants whose meanings are fixed by the combinations permitted by a formal grammar.

Logic in this sense applies to a natural language, or to a fragment of natural language, only as *formalized,* i.e., as *regimented.* From the point of view of such a conception, linguistic signs are given as syntactically marked strings independently of their employments in fact-stating discourse.

Goldfarb contrasts the schematic conception with Frege's conception, which exemplifies the *universalist conception of logic:*

There are no parts of his logical formulas that await interpretation. There is no question of providing a universe of discourse. Quantifiers in Frege's system have fixed meaning: they range over all items of the appropriate logical type (objects, one place functions of objects, two place functions of objects, etc.)[.] The letters that may figure in logical formulas, for example, in "$(p \mathrel{\&} q \rightarrow p)$" are not schematic: they are not sentence letters. Rather, Frege understands them as *variables.* Here they are free variables, and hence in accordance with Frege's general rule the formula is to be understood as a universal closure, that is, as the universally quantified statement "$(\forall p)(\forall q)(p \mathrel{\&} q \rightarrow p)$." Similarly, logical formulas containing one-place function signs are to be understood not schematically, but as generalizing over all functions. ("Frege's Conception of Logic," 67)

According to the universalist conception there is no exterior point of view on language, and so all propositions lie at the same level, including logical propositions which are propositions about reality couched in a vocabulary that is not specific to any subject matter. There is no such thing as the use of a semantic vocabulary in the characterization of propositions as logically true and of arguments as sound and valid, and signs are identified in terms of their being employed to express judgments within the contexts of inferences.

Frege sought to design a logical notation, the *Begriffsschrift*, in which the dependence of the conclusion upon the premises in all valid arguments would be made apparent. He concluded that in a notation which manifests the logical dependence of an instance on a generalization, namely, an instantiation as a valid inference, all propositional signs must display the way they are functionally composed through the application of functional expressions to argument expressions. Since all expressions are functionally composed, one can say that two expressions have the same *functional type* if they are of the same functional level and have the same number of arguments (the 0-level of functional expressions consists of proper names, which are the argument-expressions that fill first-level functional expressions). For Frege, expressions can be substituted for one another without destroying the unity of the logical whole (e.g., a propositional sign) if and only if they have the same functional type. The difference in functional type is associated, in the *Begriffsschrift*, with a difference in the style of variables. I call this a view of logical complexity the *functionalist conception*, and since whether or not an expression can instantiate a variable depends only on its functional form, the functionalist conception is universalist.

The terms that Frege uses for logical or ontological categories such as a *name, concept-word, object,* or *concept* point therefore to the differences and similarities displayed by the features of signs in the *Begriffsschrift* that manifest differences in functional form. But it can be proven that, precisely insofar as these terms indicate features of the notation, they cannot be construed as predicates in the *Begriffsschrift*, and since the notation is designed to express perspicuously all fact-stating discourse, one must come to see that in Frege's use of such terms they function merely as hints or tropes by which the use and the point of the notation are communicated to the student.

A similar point can be made with respect to Frege's use of semantic notions such as *"the sense of . . ."* and *"the reference of . . . ,"* namely, insofar as we come to see them as pointing to similarities and differences displayed by the notation, we recognize that they are not predicates, since all predicates are expressible using the notation; hence we come to see them as mere means deployed to communicate the use of the notation to a learner. In the end, the success of this communication requires this realization. One can say, therefore, that Frege's universalist conception is *eliminativist* with respect to both semantical and formal-categorical discourse. Note that the very construction of the *Begriffsschrift* is not in any obvious way internal to the fact-stating discourse, namely, we cannot describe it as the actualization of the capacity of linguistic self-consciousness which is internal to the activity of assertion as such.

In two central cases Frege proposes that a functionalist analysis can capture the use of semantic idioms in ordinary discourse. The first is the truth-connector . . . *is true,* and the second is the connector of reported discourse, e.g., . . . says that __. From the functionalist / universalist point of view the truth-connector . . . *is true* is a predicate in the object language which belongs to the same logical category as the logical connectives (in contrast to the schematic conception in which the truth predicate is metalinguistic and thus radically disguised from the logical constants that belong to the object language).

Frege argues that the truth predicate cannot express a property of propositions and concludes that it must be thought-*transparent* in the sense that the proposition p has the same sense as the proposition "p is true."[14] One can identify the truth-predicate within the *Begriffsschrift* as the content-stroke, which is a thought-transparent concept expression: (. . .), that has only the truth-value the true in its extension. (See footnote 11.)

On Frege's functionalist treatment, the connectors of ascription, e.g., __ believes . . . , are relational predicates that differ from the logical connectives in virtue of being intensional connectors—that is, by creating contexts in which words have their ordinary sense as their reference. For example, the proposition "A believes that Jacob is Joseph's father" is, according to this analysis, a *relational* proposition whose relata are A and the thought that Jacob is Joseph's father, but the fact that Jacob and Israel are identical does not license the inference to "A believes that Israel is Joseph's father," and so "Israel" in this context does not have the same reference as "Jacob."

The non-Fregean recognition of propositions as syncategorematic units leads to a different interpretation of these semantic locutions: given that

---

[14] See the discussion on Frege's three senses of truth in Chapter 3, 6.4.

propositions are syncategorematic units, the truth-connector is not a predicate, and more generally, there is no predication which is external to simple
predication. The truth-connector is therefore seen as an expression of an
operation. In fact, we can speak of truth *and* falsity operations, which are
performed by . . . *is true* and . . . *is false* respectively. The assertion "p is
true" is the same as "I truly think p." There is no logical gap between these
assertions. By contrast, the assertion "p is false" is not the same as "I truly
think not-p." Thus, truth and falsity operations are not symmetrical. However, they both apply to p and "A thinks p." It is only in judgments about
others that the use of . . . *is false* is required in addition to negation.

It follows from the recognition that simple propositions are syncategorematic units that the connectors of ascription are not predicates, and so, for
example, a thought of the form: "A believes p" is not a predication whose
subject is A, i.e., it does not represent a determination of A (instead, one can say,
it constitutes me as possibly agreeing or disagreeing with A with respect to p).

Another consequence of this recognition is that propositions occur in the
context of connectors only in one way, namely, as the basis for operations
(i.e., ascriptions in self-consciousness), and consequently there is no deep duality of intensional and extensional contexts. (I shall return to this point in
Chapter 3 in the discussion of the treatment of negation in Plato's *Sophist*.)

Consider the inference:

(1) A believes p,
(2) p
hence,
(3) A truly believes that p.

Neither Fregean functionalism nor the schematic conception can adequately show that this inference is valid.[15] Thus these conceptions do not

---

[15] A Fregean may argue that this inference is self-evident since "A truly judges p" is just
"A judges p and p" and therefore the conclusion is nothing more than a conjunction of
the premises which seen from a Fregean point of view are logically unrelated. The inadequacy of this proposal lies in the logical unrelatedness of the premises. The deflationist's construal "A truly judges p" is based here on the identification the truth-value of
the content signified by "p" in an intensional context with the truth-value of the assertion "p." I would argue that this association is arbitrary since the nameable content
cannot display an assertoric act.

allow us to identify (2), on any logical basis, as specifying the truth conditions of—or being the truth-maker of—(1). But it is a consequence of the
identification of propositions as syncategorematic that the logical unity of
(1), (2), and (3) is self-evident, which means that (2) gives the truth-conditions
of (1). We can describe this notion of the semantic, which is based on the
identification of indirect contexts and truth connectors as syncategorematic
expressions (and thus as operation signs), as *immanent* or *elucidatory seman-
tics*. Semantic clarification, from this point of view, is not external to the
fact-stating discourse: it agrees with Frege, and disagrees with the schematic
conception, in that the truth connector and the logical connectives are, *qua*
connectors, of the same logical type. But the opposite consequence is drawn
from this: whereas from the Fregean point of view, there is no such thing as
a serious semantical discourse, from the point of view the semantic immanentist, we can say that all discourse, in a sense, already includes its own
semantic self-clarification.

The immanentist view of the semantic as syncategorematic and elucida-
tive, rather than predicative, is thus distinct both from the schematic and the
universalist, eliminativist conceptions.[16]

---

[16] There is a common tendency among modern commentators to read Aristotle through the
prism of the schematic conception of logic, and to credit him with the invention of the use
of schemata and of formal languages in his characterization of the forms of syllogisms.

In a recent essay, Benjamin Morison rejects this reading of Aristotle's logic, arguing that

> Aristotle did not formalize ordinary Greek sentences into some regimented language. He
> generalizes about arguments by describing the relationship between what their premises
> and conclusion say, rather than by describing the syntactic form that the propositions would
> have to have. ("What Was Aristotle's Concept of Logical Form?," in *Episteme, etc.: Essays in
> Honour of Jonathan Barnes* [Oxford: Oxford University Press, 2011], 181)

Morison suggests that Aristotle employs a somewhat artificial Greek, consisting of letters and words nevertheless familiar to every reader of Greek, in order to spell out what the
propositions in a syllogism say in a way that clearly marks the subject and predicate term
in each proposition. The aim of Aristotle's logic is, on this reading, to display the conclusion as following from the premises through a clarificatory specification of what is said by
the premises and conclusion—that is, of their truth conditions—at the relevant level of
generality. The variables function, therefore, not as metatheoretical variables, but simply as
a means of specifying the truth conditions of judgments of the relevant generality.

Aristotle's logic, on this reading, offers a semantic elucidation of valid arguments, one
which does not involve a metatheoretical point of view. I propose that Morison's account of Aristotle's logic is best understood in light of the immanentist understanding
of semantic discourse which I would like to ascribe to Aristotle.

11. Contradictory Pairs

At *De Int.* 6, Aristotle introduces the subject of the whole treatise, the *contradictory pair (antiphasis)*:[17]

> [I]t is possible to state of what does hold that it does not hold, of what does not hold that it does hold, of what does hold that it does hold, and of what does not hold that it does not hold. Similarly for times outside the present. So it must be possible to deny whatever anyone has affirmed, and to affirm whatever anyone has denied. Thus it is clear that for every affirmation there is an opposite negation, and for every negation an opposite affirmation. Let us call an affirmation and a negation which are opposite a contradiction. (17a26–37)

Whitaker paraphrases these remarks as follows:

> A simple assertion claims either that something holds or that it does not hold (17a23 f.); these assertions are affirmations and negations (17a25 f.). Since anything which holds can be said to hold or not to hold, and the same may also be said of anything which does not hold, it is quickly concluded that everything that can be affirmed can be denied, and vice versa (17a26–31). Thus, all affirmations and negations are paired off with one another: to every affirmation there is a negation, and to every negation an affirmation (17a31–3). In any such pair, the affirmation represents something as holding, while the negation represents it as not holding. Having arrived at this result,

---

[17] *De Interpretatione* is traditionally taken to be a study of assertions in general, i.e., *logoi apophantikoi.* Recently, however, C. W. A. Whitaker has contested this assumption, arguing that the topic is *contradictory pairs* of assertions. And since (he says) Aristotle holds that contradictory pairs play a central role in dialectic but not in other rational inquiries, a major purpose of *De Interpretatione* is to lay the ground for works such as the *Topica* and the *Sophistici Elenchi,* which deal with the asking and answering of dialectical questions with a view to refuting a thesis. Thus, Whitaker finds the traditional title inapt

> whether taken to mean "On the Assertion," or, as on Waitz's view "On Communication" or "On Language." The title is not supported in other works of Aristotle, and should be rejected as spurious. *"On the Contradictory Pair"* would be the most obvious title to express the true subject of the treatise. (Whitaker, *Aristotle's De Interpretatione,* 7)

In a recent essay, Walter Leszl argues convincingly that Whitaker understates the breadth of the discussion in *De Interpretatione* by disregarding the role that contradictory pairs play in all forms of discursive activity:

Aristotle defines a new term, that is, the contradictory pair *(antiphasis)*, consisting of the affirmation and the negation which are opposed to each other
(17a33 f.). He also stipulates that the two contradictory assertions must op-
pose each other in the same sense: contradiction which depends on hom-
onymy and other sophistries does not count as genuine (17a34–7). (*Aristotle's De Interpretatione*, 78–79)

The argument, as Whitaker understands it, rests on a distinction between the *force* and *content* of a simple judgment. The content is something
that can hold or fail to hold, and also something that can be held to hold
or held not to hold. On this reading, the argument does not depend on
whether the content in question is taken as a propositional content or as a
predicative content. However, the context suggests that the argument
deals with something that holds or fails to hold *concerning the subject,* and
therefore that the content in question is predicative. The two contradictory
acts are therefore describable as an affirmation and the denial that some-

Whitaker can . . . be accused of . . . narrowness . . . when he posits as an alternative for investigation assertion and the contradictory pair, assuming that the latter can be of interest
only for a study which offers the "theoretical background for dialectic," while assertion as
the basic element of the syllogism is of interest for the analytics. When one looks at what
Aristotle has to say about the premise, one general definition he gives of it is as follows:
"A premise is one or the other part of a contradiction, one thing said of one, dialectical if it
takes indifferently either part, demonstrative if it determinately [takes] the one that is true"
(*Apo.* I 2, 72a8–11). In the first chapter of the *Prior Analytics* one meets a similar formulation,
as follows: "A demonstrative premise is different from a dialectical one in that a demonstrative
premise is the taking of one or the other part of a contradiction (for someone who is demon-
strating does not ask for premises but takes them), whereas a dialectical premise is the asking
of a contradiction. . . ." This passage shows that Aristotle did not suppose there is any fundamental difference, from a logical point of view, between the deduction of the one who demonstrates and the deduction of the one who argues dialectically. . . . [H]e thought that even the
one who demonstrates has an alternative before him, that is to say, gives a tacit reply to a [yes-
no] question he sets himself, but, before coming to the demonstration, must have reached a
decision by exclusion of "one part of the contradiction" (possibly on the basis of some evidence, anyhow because he believes it is false). It would be strange if science, at the stage of
doing research, excluded asking questions and adopting one of the two parts of the contradiction which is envisaged by each question that is asked. It could be added that Aristotle is in-
clined to see some affinity between affirmation and negation in the case of thought and pursuit and avoidance in the case of wish, cf. *Nicomachean Ethics,* VI 2, 1139a21 ff., and *De
Anima* III 7, 431a9–10, and that he often asserts that knowledge of opposites is the same. All
this tends to suggest that for him when one makes a judgment one has in mind not just
the simple assertion or the simple negation but makes a sort of choice between the two.
(Walter Leszl, "Aristotle's Logical Works and His Conception of Logic," *Topoi* 23 [2004]:
71–100, 94)

thing, i.e., a predicative content, holds concerning the subject. The description of affirmation and negation in terms of an assertoric (predicative) act and content is taken as proof that for any simple affirmation there is a single act which is its negation, and vice versa. It is precisely this kind of dualist reading of the passage that I wish to reject by instead proposing that the passage introduces contradictory pairs through a semantic clarification of affirmation and negation.

On the dualistic construal, truth and falsity belong to the content of a simple judgment independently of the logical unity of affirmation and denial. I shall argue, however, that this notion of content and the associated construal of judgment / assertion is incoherent, and moreover that it is wrong to ascribe it to Aristotle, for whom the basic locus of truth and falsity is in a contradictory pair of judgments.

12. The Challenge

Aristotle gives three characterizations of affirmation and negation with a view to elucidating the difference between the positive and negative members of a simple contradictory pair. (See Table 2.1.)

(1), (2), and (3) are widely read as being simply different expressions for the same categorematic distinction between two ways of bringing a subject and a predicate term into a propositional unity.

That contradictory pairs should be characterized categorematically follows directly from *semantic compositionalism*—viz., the thesis that the semantic value of a complex expression is determined by the semantic value of the components and their manner of composition. Since the members of a contradictory pair have opposite truth values if their components are the

---

There are different ways of thinking of a judgment as a choice between affirmation and denial. For example, the choice might be taken as analogous to a choice between two roads at a fork. This analogy fails, however, because it is possible to continue down one of the roads without noticing the other, whereas it is not possible to make a positive judgment without being aware of it as one member of a pair. In other words, each of the two contradictory acts must be essentially two-in-one; the choice of either must contain the pair. Unfortunately, Leszl does not provide an account of this two-in-oneness, and thus it is not clear from his discussion how the analogy of avoidance and pursuit could shed light on the duality of affirmation and denial.

Table 2.1

Affirmation	*Negation*
1. Stating of something that it holds	Stating of something that it does not hold
2. Asserting toward something	Asserting away from something
3. Combination	Separation

same, semantic compositionalism holds that their manner of composition must be different.

This, however, is wrong—or so I will argue. We must therefore search for a characterization of contradictory pairs that goes beyond the alternatives dictated by the compositionalist thesis.[18] In other words, we must try to comprehend the different characterizations listed here, and in particular *combination* and *separation,* as clarifying a *syncategorematic* difference between positive and negative contradictory acts.

13. Propositional Unity: Functionalism and Factualism

In Plato's *Sophist* the Eleatic Stranger teaches the young Theaetetus that we do not "say" *(legein)* something through a name *(onoma)* or a verb *(rhêma)* alone—but only through their combination (262d4–5). He calls such combination "the simplest *logos*" (262d5–6).

Some philosophers detect an explanatory gap in these remarks, one that needs to be filled by an account that identifies the source which is able to distinguish the list of expressions that make up the *logos* from the simple *logos* itself. The problem is that attempts to ground the unity of a proposition by invoking a combining nexus lead to a vicious regress or circle (sometimes known as Bradley's regress). The philosophical quietist with respect to the problem of the unity of proposition rejects this explanatory demand by noting that it arises only from the illusion that propositional components

---

[18] Given the compositionalist assumption, the contradictory difference can only be a difference (i) in the form or mode of composition, (ii) in the significance of propositional components, or (iii) in assertoric force. It is a useful exercise to go through each of these to show how any compositionalist interpretation of the contradictory difference as categorematic leads to a dead end.

are given independently of their role in propositions and thus discursive activity. In fact, since the quietist subscribes to the context principle, propositions are indefinable and are internally articulated by their place within a larger discursive context. For Frege, this larger context is that of inferential activity, which for him is the activity of making judgments on the basis of other judgments in accordance with logical norms. I take it that Wittgenstein and Aristotle see the larger context to which a judgment belongs as the unity of consciousness and language use. I shall show that the two views of the discursive context in which judgments (constitutively) inhere correspond to radically different conceptions of the distinctive unity and inner articulation of a proposition, i.e., the *logos,* as that which can be true or false: the first is Fregean functionalism, and the second can be described as noncompositionalist factualism.

The more familiar factualist conception of predicative unity is, in fact, *compositionalist-factualism (c-factualism)* which is commonly—though I believe wrongly—associated with Wittgenstein's *Tractatus,* and which was adopted in some form by Wilfrid Sellars on the basis of what I take to be a misreading of that work.

From a functionalist point of view, a simple propositional sign is a complex entity, and given the context principle, the identification of a component in a proposition, e.g., a name or a predicate, is a description of the complex that tracks its possibilities of occurrence in valid arguments.

By contrast, factualism is the view that a propositional sign is a determination of the names in it, and thus a proposition is the fact that, as components of the propositional sign, the name or names stand in a certain way.[19]

---

[19] Within functionalism, complete expressions are formally indistinguishable insofar as any two names or singular terms are intersubstitutable, and therefore we can say that all complete expressions have the form that is associated with a variable in a first-level function. By contrast, according to factualism, different names may be distinguished by their forms. Two names have the same form if what can be said about one can be said about the other, in other words, if they are determined in the same ways. The form of a name reflects the form of the name-bearer, namely, the ways the name-bearer can be. Thus, in factualism but not functionalism, a notion of a form of a particular belongs to logic itself.

One of the main weaknesses of Aristotle's logical work, from a Fregean point of view, is the gap it opens between scientific knowledge of generalizations and empirical knowledge of singular propositions. Frege's logical work is designed to admit inferences that result in knowledge of particulars, namely, in singular judgments. But it can be

Therefore, a recognition of propositional complexity, according to the factualist, is a judgment concerning names and is not primarily about the complexes in which the names occur.

In distinguishing functionalism from factualism I am appealing to the distinction between a *complex* and a *fact*. A *complex* has an internal articulation, the parts and the whole of which can play the role of subject in various kinds of predication. By contrast, the internal articulation of a *fact* is displayed or revealed by a true predication. But we can only come to recognize this difference in its full radicality once we recognize that *facts* are syncategorematic units. Indeed, at this point of the dialectic, the difference between *functionalism* and *factualism* cannot be sufficiently clarified—it will only emerge fully once we come to see factualism in its noncompositionalist form.

Consider the example of two propositions that share a predicate:

(1) Diotima is wise.
(2) Socrates is wise.

From the functionalist point of view (1) and (2) are complexes of the same type. There are various ways of describing this common type in the literature: we can follow Geach in describing (1) and (2) as supplying values of the same propositional functor__ *is wise* for the names "Diotima" and "Socrates." Or we can speak, with Frege, of the completion of the functional expression __ *is wise* by the names "Diotima" and "Socrates." The functionalist maintains that the common character of the complexes reflects their common logical role in inferences—in this case we recognize that both are possible premises of a valid inference to the general conclusion $(\exists x)$ $(x$ is wise).

From the factualist point of view, (1) and (2) are two determinations of names that share a predicate insofar as the name "Diotima" is determined in propositional sign (1) in the same way that the name "Socrates" is determined in propositional sign (2). One can say that in both cases the name is flanked to the right by the expression . . . *is wise*. The judgment about the names by which the predicative form of the propositional sign is stated is similar in

---

argued that Frege is simply changing the subject, since he cannot not capture in his logic the generality of Aristotelian categorical propositions, nor the particularity of Aristotelian singular propositions. One can hope to show that, since on the factualist account particulars have forms, this account can capture both particularity and generality in a way that does not create the problem of a logical gap between generalizations and singular propositions, while admitting the possibility of privation relative to the form.

THE DOMINANT SENSE OF BEING

form to the judgment about the name-bearers which is displayed by the propositional sign.

These two accounts of predicative unity appear to suffer from opposite shortcomings: while factualism is too narrow, functionalism is too broad. *Factualism* only provides a treatment of positive predication, with no clear way to extend this to compound propositions or even to negation. *Functionalism* treats all logically complex expressions on a par, since it views them as functionally equivalent. But for that reason, it can be shown to lack the resources required to mark the distinctive logical character of concept-words (predicates) as special first-order functional expressions that are incomplete components of propositions.

In what follows, I will suggest that factualism, but not functionalism, can be emended in a way that will allow us to make sense of the contradictory difference as syncategorematic. At that point, I will distinguish *compositionalist factualism* (c-factualism) from a noncompositionalist form of factualism that I shall call *propositional factualism* (p-factualism). It will become clear that there cannot be an analogous distinction between c-functionalism and p-functionalism. But before I can do this, I have to say more about c-factualism and functionalism.

14. *So they look on ideas as dumb pictures on a tablet, and misled by this preconception they fail to see that an idea, insofar as it is an idea, involves affirmation or negation.* (B. Spinoza, *Ethics* II, 49)

Aristotle's account of truth and falsity, in Theta 10 and elsewhere, is often read as a kind of a picture theory, according to which a combination (or separation) of terms constituting a judgment is an isomorphic image of a situation (i.e., fact or state of affairs) in reality—that is, of a combination (or separation) of the significations of the terms. There are, in fact, both c-factualist and functionalist versions of the picture theory.[20] According

[20] On the face of it, Fregean functionalism appears to be incompatible with picture theories. The reference (i.e., *Bedeutung*) of a proposition, according to Frege, is a truth-value, which is a simple object, and therefore a proposition cannot be described as an isomorphic image of its reference. Furthermore, there is a technical argument, known in the literature as the *slingshot argument,* which purports to prove that introducing another functionalist notion of propositional reference will not help, since, given

to the c-factualist picture theory, the truth or falsity of a proposition, which is a combination of names, depends on the corresponding combination of name-bearers.

A consequence of the picture theory is that all meaningful propositions, not just true ones, are isomorphic images of states of affairs. Since a proposition can be *either* true or false, being true cannot simply be a matter of depicting a state of affairs—of being an isomorphic image of a state of affairs.

This might be thought to suggest[21] that the truth or falsehood of a simple affirmation or denial—i.e., of a combination or separation—consists in the obtaining or non-obtaining of the state of affairs depicted by them. A combination, on this suggestion, would represent what it depicts as obtaining, while a separation would represent the same combination as non-obtaining. But a simple affirmation and its contradictory counterpart depict the same state of affairs. Therefore, the difference between obtaining and non-obtaining, and so between simple affirmation and denial, must be merely syncategorematic.

This suggestion is based on a dualism of force and content, since it is committed to the notion that truth and falsity inhere in the content of an

---

simple compositionalist assumptions concerning substitution, if propositions have any reference, then all true (or all false) propositions have the same reference.

John McDowell, for one, dismisses this argument as philosophically irrelevant by presenting the world / reality as the realm of senses:

> The *Sinn* expressed in assertoric utterance is what one says in making the utterance. What one says is, schematically, that things are thus and so, and that things are thus and so is what is the case, if one's assertion is true. And something that is the case is, in a quite intuitive way of speaking, a state of affairs. So an intuitive notion of states of affairs is perfectly available to Frege, but in the realm of *Sinn* rather than *Bedeutung*. ("Evan's Frege," in *The Engaged Intellect* [Cambridge, MA: Harvard University Press, 2009], 176)

On the deflationist picture theory that McDowell endorses, *a true proposition* mirrors a state of affairs—its content—which is the case. One objection which can be brought against a functionalist picture theory of this kind is that states of affairs which inhere in the world are too language-like, insofar as the content of the following two claims: (1) *a is bigger than b*, and (2) *b is smaller than a* cannot be identified as only formally different. The factualist picture theory does not suffer from a similar problem, since (1) and (2) can be identified as merely formally different. Ironically, the functionalist picture theory is vulnerable to the objection that it makes facts too language-like precisely because it is based on a notion of sense which is independent of language.

[21] For a proposal along these lines, see Hans Johan Glock, "Truth in the Tractatus," *Synthese*, 148 (2006): 345–368.

affirmation or a denial independently of their contradictory unity. The syn-categorematic bipolarity of obtaining and non-obtaining is extrinsic to the state of affairs itself.

Consider therefore the *dual counterpart* of a state of affairs, which differs from the original state of affairs only insofar as the obtaining (or non-obtaining) of the counterpart is the same as the non-obtaining (or obtaining) of the original. There cannot be anything in a simple affirmation that determines whether the state of affairs it depicts is the original or the counterpart. Hence, it is meaningless to describe affirmation or denial as true or false. We can conclude that the suggestion provides only an illusion of understanding.

I would argue that Aristotle's remarks on truth and falsity in Theta 10 and elsewhere are not expressions of this illusion, yet Aristotle's use of the term *logos apophantikos* contains a certain insight into the revelatory character of propositions that needs to be distinguished from this illusion through a correct understanding of factualism.

15. p-Factualism and c-Factualism

TLP 3.1432 is often taken as evidence of Wittgenstein's factualism, which is widely construed as c-factualism:

> Not: "The complex sign *'aRb'* says that *a* stands in the relation *R* to *b*," but: *That "a"* stands in a certain relation to *"b"* says *that aRb.*

"___ says *that p*" can be taken as equivalent to "___ *displays the judgment* or *assertion that p.*" *TLP* 3.1432 would then say: *that "a"* stands in a certain relation to *"b"* displays the judgment *that aRb.*

But I do not think it is either helpful or necessary to read this as a statement of c-factualism. It is not helpful because c-factualism is a bad theory. And it is not necessary because another reading is possible.

From the c-factualist point of view a simple proposition gives a spatial model of a situation. Consider, for example, the diagram:

(I) <u>C</u>

Suppose the letter *C* stands for a cat, while the underlying bar stands for a mat; if the placing of one name above another is associated with the first name-bearer being on top of the second, then the configuration of C and _ in (I) might be taken as a model of the state or situation *cat being on a mat*.

But (I), understood isomorphically, can be used to make two contradictory claims. One can say that the pair *(cat, mat) are thus* (as in (I)), or alternatively that the pair *(cat, mat) are* not *thus* (as in (I)). The placing of C above _ cannot be identified with one of these claims rather than the other.

This shows that the c-factualist lacks the means to describe the propositional sign *"aRb"* as displaying a judgment, for he cannot say why the *fact that "a"* stands in a *certain relation* to *"b"* (flanking R from left to right) displays *"that aRb"* rather than its contradictory. Consequently, c-factualism fails as a theory of judgment.

There is another way to bring this out: a proposition and its negation do not display contradictory judgments as two distinct spatial models. Rather, the negation is symbolized by the negation sign, which as a sign is not part of another spatial model. Hence, the difference between a simple proposition and its negation is not a spatial difference between two spatial models. For example, (1) *Theaetetus is flying* and (2) *Theaetetus is not flying* display contradictory judgments, but not in virtue of being two contrasting determinations of "Theaetetus," i.e., not in virtue of any categorematic difference. Rather, the difference between (1) and (2) is syncategorematic, so that (1) occurs in (2), without there being any extra categorematic content to (2) over and above that which is provided it by the occurrence of (1).

According to what I will call *p-factualism*, a simple propositional sign both depicts (reveals) a possible determination of name bearers by being a determination of their names, while also being negatable. Moreover, p-factualism holds that these two roles cannot be dissociated. We shall conclude that since positive predication is dominated by the syncategorematic unity of the contradictory pair, picture theory in the sense of c-factualism is false. Yet because positive predication is prior, and because there is no predicative content to negative predication over and above that which is provided it by the occurrence of the positive predication within it, picture theory, in the sense of p-factualism, is correct.

Read as a statement of p-factualism, the left side of the proposition (*) *"That 'a' stands in a certain relation to 'b' says that aRb"* is a self-ascription of a simple positive predication, i.e., a judgment about a and b, on the basis of a judgment concerning the way the names *"a"* and *"b"* occur within the propositional sign that expresses this judgment.

In fact (*) is a proposition of the form: "*p* says that *p*"; given that *p* is a simple proposition, "*p*" is an ascription / identification of an assertion / judgment about objects on the basis of a judgment about the names within the propositional sign which express that judgment.

Thus, the subject of the act in the left side of (*) can be made explicit by the expression: I ("*aRb*"), which means that I ascribe to myself the judgment / assertion that aRb on the basis of a similar judgment concerning the names: "*a*" *R*-left-flanks "*b*." I ascribe to myself the judgment *aRb* through a judgment about "*a*" and "*b*" which is "*aRb*," and both judgments have the same form.

On this reading, "*aRb*" specifies / ascribes a judgment / assertion (about a and b) via a propositional fact, i.e., it is stated by a judgment (about "*a*" and "*b*"). As such, "*aRb*" is internally related to the judgment / assertion *aRb* in the following way: 1. A ("*aRb*"), 2. *aRb*, therefore 3. A truly ("*aRb*"). This inference has a similar form to the inference: 1. A believes *p*, 2. *p*, and therefore 3. A truly believes *p*.

Therefore, "-*aRb*" specifies / ascribes a negative judgment / assertion (about a and b) by a propositional fact stated by a judgment (about "*a*" and "*b*").

This inference shows that the quotation employed in 3.1432 ascribes an act via the propositional fact, and hence does so without isolating and killing the sign by an external metatheoretical semantic assent.

According to p-factualism, there is a crucial asymmetry between the positive and negative predications. While the positive proposition depicts or reveals how things are determined if it is true, and displays the judgment (viz., *says*) that they are so determined (see, e.g., *TLP* 4.022), the negative proposition depicts or reveals how things are if it is *false* and displays the judgment (viz., *says*) that they are *not* so determined. The positive and negative simple proposition, affirmation and negation, can thus be glossed as pointing toward and away from the determination revealed by the positive proposition. The notion of a difference between two directions is used here as a figure for a syncategorematic difference. It is important not to read this figure literally, since the differences in spatial direction are categorematic. Indeed, all attempts to elucidate syncategorematic differences must appeal to categorematic distinctions and should therefore be approached with similar caution.

We can now, in light of p-factualism, recognize the wrongness of the c-factualist conception of spatial models themselves. The c-factualist's appeal to spatial models as capable of displaying, in a primitive manner, the way that propositional signs are supposed to represent, rests on a misunderstanding of the use of a complex of items as a representation, i.e., a model. In fact, in seeing a complex as a model, we incorporate it into a negatable proposition of the form: things stand *thus* ("*thus*" is to be understood as latching onto the complex here). Hence, spatial models cannot be taken as primitive representations that, through their simplicity, disclose the nature of propositional representations.

It is also wrong to describe a contradictory pair as consisting of two contrasting uses of one spatial model—that affirmation and negation use the same proposition to say how things are and how they are not. This suggests, incorrectly, that the proposition by itself is directionless or dissociated from force, and that its direction is added to it by the positive or negative use.

Once Aristotle's account of the *logos apophantikos* is read as p-factualist, the following of its features make sense: (1) the priority of affirmation to negation, along with the dominance of the contradictory pair, (2) the priority of both to compound propositions, along with the dominance of the compound, and finally (3) the revealing character of simple affirmations and negations in contrast to the nonrevealing character of compound propositions.

We can now classify judgments according to their representational purport in the following way. While simple affirmation, but not simple negation, represents an object or objects as being determined in a certain way, we can nonetheless describe both as representations that are revealing of an object. By contrast, a conjunction of representations of an object should not be described as a representation of an object, since the conjuncts can be representations of different objects. We can describe conjunctions as representations of the world. The world, understood as the togetherness of facts (both positive and negative), is co-signified by the operation of conjunction. As a possible conjunct, any representation of an object is also a representation of the world, that is, a claim about the world. It is worth mentioning here that judgments of the form "I think *p*" or "A thinks *p*" are not representations of the world—indeed, I think that it would be misleading to call such judgments representations of any kind.

16. A Note on the Verb

According to p-factualism, the verb in a simple proposition is a way of holding / combining one or several singular terms, one which displays the judgment / assertion that the objects signified by these terms are similarly held / thus combined. The separation which is the negation of the verb is not a different combination, i.e., a different way of holding the terms; instead it is a *separation* of the combination associated with the verb, in the sense that it displays the assertion that the object or objects signified are not similarly combined.

The verb, understood as a way of holding or combining names / singular terms in a simple proposition, has a liminal being: it lies between the categorematic and the syncategorematic. On the one hand, the verb is categorematic since it is internal to the simple positive proposition; but on the other hand, as the negatable part of a proposition, it is the locus of the syncategorematic difference.

Aristotle distinguishes, in *De Interpreatione,* the *verb* as it occurs in singular propositions, from the *name,* by two marks: firstly, a name is without time, whereas a verb signifies time in addition (that is, it cosignifies time) (16b6); and secondly, a verb is "a sign of things said of the subject" (16b7). In other words, a verb is distinguished from a name insofar as (1) it cosignifies tense, (2) it signifies something that is said of the subject, that is, a possible determination of the subject.

These two marks of verbs are intimately related: by using the idiom *signifying in addition* or *cosignifying,* Aristotle is conveying that time is not signified by anything categorematic in the *logos,* but rather by its syncategorematic unity, i.e., by the combination.[22] Tense, therefore, is not signified, but is

---

[22] Tense is co-signified by the verb in a simple proposition. It is useful to compare this account with that of Sebastian Rödl's *Categories of the Temporal: An Inquiry into the Forms of the Finite Intellect* (Cambridge MA: Harvard University Press, 2008). One of Rödl's basic insights is that there is no logical gap between the judgment that *p* and the assessment of this judgment as true. The immediate consequence is that a judgment is not assessed as true or false relative to a context or situation; to think otherwise is to introduce a logical gap between judging and the assessment of the judgment "as the latter would have to refer the judgment to the relevant circumstances" (60).

Since the veridical verbs (". . . is the case," ". . . is true") do not apply relative to a context or a time, Rödl concludes that they apply absolutely—*timelessly*—to thoughts (i.e., to judgeable contents).

But the conclusion only seems necessary because Rödl assumes that veridical verbs have the logical character of predicates or *determination words*. In fact, I would suggest, his insight shows that they are *not* determination words—they are not categorematic. Rather, they are *syncategorematic* expressions for operations. And it is meaningless to view such expressions as either relative or absolute determinations *of* veridical beings.

Yet, Rödl is correct that the truth of a judgment is independent of anything external to it. Indeed, a judgment does not depend for its success on anything external to it.

cosignified—it is syncategorematic. Similarly, I would argue, the *logos* co-signifies rather than signifies the judging subject (i.e., the "I") and the world. The combination which is a positive fact (e.g., that Socrates is sitting) is revealed by a true *logos*, whereas the act or determination within such a combination is signified by the verb in a *logos*.

17. Combination as a Capacity and an Act

In *Metaphysics* Theta 2 Aristotle characterizes a rational capacity (*dunamis meta logou,* a capacity that has to do with a *logos*) as a two-way capacity, and contrasts it with a nonrational, or one-way, capacity. The description of the difference between, and the unity of, affirmation and negation suggests that they stand to one another as contrasting acts of a two-way capacity.

A rational capacity is one that a rational agent can possess as such. The example Aristotle gives is a medical skill, which is an understanding of health and, with it, the ability to work to produce and preserve the healthy condition of the body. It is a two-way capacity insofar as the same understanding and ability can be used to destroy health with special effectiveness.

The capacity can be identified with the existence in the soul of an understanding of a form that can originally inform beings (e.g., health). It is a two-way capacity insofar as it can be active in (i) productively bringing about or preserving the form in something and (ii) in destructively removing the form from something. In other words, a two-way capacity is for forming and

---

This insight is precisely that of the sameness of thinking and being. But the significance of this insight is lost if we do not distinguish the categorematic from the syncategorematic.

But since Rödl concludes that veridical verbs apply absolutely, he needs to explain how *situational thoughts* are even possible. How can a judgment arise from the experience of an object in time? There seems to be a tension between the insight that thinking and being are the same and the notion that an empirical judgment depends on a particular object in a particular situation.

Rödl tries to resolve this tension by distinguishing two notions of logic and of logical form: a *logical-transcendental form*, which characterizes the situational dependency of situational thoughts, and a *logical-inferential* form associated with the ways the thought can occur within a valid argument. Rödl holds that a speaker asserts something using a situational *sentence in virtue of the time of the assertion*. Nonetheless, what gets asserted must be independent of that particular time, since it can also be asserted at other times. What I asserted last week with the sentence "*S* is *F*" I can also assert today with "*S was F*," and tomorrow, and so forth.

deforming according to a form that can itself be said to have a direction (i.e., a form of unity).

The two capacities are not symmetrical with respect to their two activities, since the capacity is directed toward the positive act, e.g., medical skill is a skill for healing, not for harming. We can say that harming is the privative act of the two-way capacity.

Viewed as a two-way capacity, a simple propositional sign is a capacity with two activities: combination and separation. The capacity itself can be described as a capacity for combination, i.e., for holding the name in a certain way. The term *combination* is thus used for the capacity associated with a simple propositional sign and for its positive act.

Let us recall that the negative act, viz., separation, is the identification of consciousness as disagreeing with the positive act. As the act of a two-way capacity, it is performed on the basis of a display of *combination,* as an identification of consciousness in terms of what it disagrees with. Separation can therefore be described as a separation from the combination, but which is itself an act of the combination.

Situational sentences are interrelated in such a way that a sentence can express the same thought on one occasion that a different sentence, associated with the first, expresses on another occasion. Rödl associates the consciousness of the time from which one judges, and about which one judges, with the capacity to keep track of a thought through different linguistic expressions. His view is an example of a partial linguistic turn.

Rödl argues that the categorical distinction between substance and state is a difference in logical-transcendental form. It is within this form that he locates the difference in tense:

Substance and state . . . unite in such a way that the substance either is or was in the state. This form of thought contains a contrast; it is divided within itself. (131)

Rödl sees that "*S* is *F*" and "*S* was *F*" exhibit the same form—and indeed the same content, for the predicative unity expressed by "is" and "was" is not an element of their content. Yet he fails to recognize the difference between them as syncategorematic, and concludes that the difference reflects a distinction *within* the categorematic form. (In this sense, he proposes, it is like the sexual difference within a species: a distinction in the form that is not a formal difference.)

Note that Rödl's puzzle is the Parmendian puzzle: how can being and thinking be the same if we can think of what is not—e.g., the past? Rödl tries to deal with the puzzle by distinguishing the content of a judgment from the different ways it is available by propositional signs. He holds that what brings together the statement "*S* is *F*" made yesterday and the statement "*S* was *F*" made today is the sameness of content rather than the logical unity of thinking. Thus Rödl ignores the straightforward inferences:

The p-factualist understanding of contradictory difference is captured by its characterization of a simple contradictory pair as consisting in contrasting acts of a two-way capacity: combination and separation, where combination is displayed by the verb. The use of the Aristotelian term helps in illuminating the unity—the oneness and twoness—of two contradictory simple judgments, and it serves to clarify Aristotle's claim in *De Anima* 3.6 that the combination in the *logos* is simultaneously a separation. However, as we noted in Chapter 1, there is a deep disanalogy between the *technai,* which are the capacities which Aristotle describes as the two-way capacities, and the *logos.* The act of a *techne,* e.g., building, is expressed by a verb, whereas a judgment / assertion is not expressible by a verb but only by a proposition as whole. We must therefore agree that the assertion / judgment p is not an act, but is rather a syncategorematic act, and similarly we must say that the two-way capacity p is not a capacity but a syncategorematic capacity.[23]

(*) I truly thought that S is F. Hence, S was F.

(**) I thought that S will be F. S is F. Hence, I was right in thinking that S will be F.

For the validity of such inferences cannot be captured within a Fregean framework.

To capture these inferences we need to see that the verb in a proposition *co-signifies* time. The difference between "S is F" and "S was F" is not predicative. In particular, "S was F" does not express a *way* that S is F. Instead we should say that the difference between "S is F" and "S was F" is syncategorematic—like the difference between "S is F" and "S is not-F." The tense or time is co-signified by the proposition as a whole, and thus syncategorematically.

Thus we need to recognize (1) "S is F" occurs within (2) "S was F" insofar as (2) is the result of an operation on the basis of the gesture "S is F." We must therefore regard (1) and thus the present tense as prior, but (1) must be seen as essentially displaying a claim that can also be displayed within the "was" in (2). In other words: though the judgment "S is F" is prior to the judgment "S was F" or "S will be F," the syncategorematic unity of the three tenses associated with this judgment is dominant.

A true assertion of "S is F" reveals or represents the state of affairs that S is F. The judgment "S was F" is not similarly revelatory or representational. It is simply a way of identifying one's own consciousness as disagreeing with the judgment: "it was never correct to think 'S is F.'" Note, that the "now" according to this understanding is only available in judging. That is, it is only available logically or syncategorematically through the unity of judgment. There is no "sideways on" grasp of the present. As such, it is therefore mistaken to look for an understanding of time in physics or the philosophy of nature.

[23] Aristotle's characterization of the *technai* as capacities *meta-logou* (pertaining to the *logos*) suggests that the two-wayness of these capacities rests on the syncategorematic

18. The *Apophantik* Account of Truth and Falsity

Aristotle's account of the truth and falsity of simple propositions can be described as *apophantik*. The *apophantik account* of truth and falsity admits both judgments/propositions and facts as veridical beings, but denies that truth is a matter of a *relation* between them. Indeed, judgments and facts are syncategorematic units, so they cannot be *relata* at all.

The distinction between judgments and facts is reflected in the form of the following inferences:

(T1) *S is F.*   (F1) *S is not F.*
(T2) A thinks *that S is F.*   (F2) A thinks *that S is F.*
(T3) *Thus,* A truly thinks *that S is F.*   (F3) *Thus,* A falsely thinks *that S is F.*

The same combination occurs as the positive fact (T1) and in the judgment in (T2); the difference between (T1) and (T2) is merely syncategorematic. Similarly, the same combination occurs as a negative fact, i.e., a separation, in (F1) and in the judgment in (F2); again, the difference between (F1) and (F2) is merely syncategorematic.

It follows, according to the *apophantik* account, that the two-way capacity *S is F* can be active in the soul or in the world both positively and negatively—i.e., as combination or as separation. The positive activity of the capacity in the soul is the judgment that *S is F;* the negative activity of the capacity is the judgment that *S is not F.* The positive activity of the capacity in the world is the fact that *S is F;* the negative activity is the negative fact that *S is not F.* A judgment is true when it is an activity of a capacity in the soul that is active in the same direction in the world; a judgment is false

---

two-wayness of the *logos.* In general, thinking about human beings involves constitutive crossings of the syncategorematic / categorematic borders. For example, the syncategorematic "I" constitutively latches onto a proper name of the "I," so that in a sense, "I" needs to be determined by name. A proper name, e.g., IK, is an expression which is constitutively related to a self-identification of the form "I am IK." Such an identification, I want to argue, is not an identity proposition. Similarly, I am determined without being predicatively subsumed under "I-sorters," such as *"I am human."* Thus, the syncategorematic use of "I" cannot be isolated from the use of categorematic expressions, with which it interacts. I make these inchoate observations here partly as a call for the philosophical investigation of the unity of self-consciousness and language, e.g., proper names, within the framework of the full or complete linguistic turn.

when it is an activity of a capacity in the soul that is active in the opposite direction in the world.

We can now take up the argument that introduces contradictory pairs in *De Int.* 6 without ascribing to Aristotle a distinction between force and content. Aristotle's point is that the same *combination* that holds or does not hold in reality can also be held to hold or not to hold by the subject. A combination is held to hold by the judging subject as a combination (affirmation), and it is held not to hold as a separation (denial).

19. The Puzzles Surrounding Theta 10 (The Cross-Categorematic and the Syncategorematic)

I would like to show that the *apophantik* account of truth allows us to resolve the puzzles surrounding the opening passage of *Metaphysics* Theta 10 with which we began.

The first puzzle is in the relation of this passage to an earlier discussion in *Metaphysics* Epsilon 4 in which being in the sense of being-true is put aside as irrelevant to the concerns of first philosophy, since truth does *not* belong to things but to thought *(diainoia).*

Heidegger proposed to resolve the puzzle by disambiguating *being-true* and thereby distinguishing the topic of Epsilon 4 from that of Theta 10. Epsilon 4 deals, according to this proposal, with the being-true of predicative judgments; whereas Theta 10 by contrast deals with being the case, namely, with the being of facts. Kahn similarly sought to distinguish the topics of Epsilon 4 and Theta 10 by pointing to an ambiguity in the use of the veridical verb which, he says, may be taken to have in its extension "either the intentional content of such a predicative claim—the fact as asserted in judgment or discourse—or the objective correlate, the actual fact or state of the world that makes the claim true" ("Parmenides and Plato Once More," in *Essays on Being*, 198).

Kahn maintains that the veridical use of the verb rests on an assumption that there exists a correspondence between true truth-bearers and facts. He therefore thinks that the difference between Theta 10 and Epsilon 4 is between the two sides of the correspondence relation, namely, between truth-bearers and truth-makers.

It is a consequence of the correspondence theory of truth that the transition from the judgment *p* to the judgment *p is true* is substantive, that is, the fact acknowledged by the second judgment is categorematically different from the one acknowledged by the first. Geach points to this as sufficient grounds for rejecting the correspondence theory of truth:

> For suppose A judges that Jupiter is round: call this judgment J_1. If A reflects minimally, A will also be able to judge: My judgment that Jupiter is round is true; call this judgment J_2. J_1 and J_2 clearly stand, and indeed both stand, together: they are not made true on two different accounts. Given that J_2 is a first-person judgment simultaneous with J_1 . . . A who judges J_1 needs no further justification, no additional data, to go on to J_2. But on the theory of truth as correspondence to facts J_1's truth would be its correspondence to the roundness of Jupiter, and J_2's truth would be its correspondence to a quite different fact, namely, J_1's correspondence to the roundness of Jupiter. This is good enough reason to reject the theory; all the same, . . . it has taught us something: an adequate theory of truth must pass the test that this theory failed, namely, that J_1 and J_2 are made true in the same way and not on different accounts." (Peter Geach, "Truth and God," 84)

Geach makes this observation in support of Frege's position that . . . *is true* is *sui generis* in not expressing a property, and thus in being sense-transparent. But our discussion shows that the conclusion that needs to be drawn from Geach's observation is that the difference between J_1 and J_2 is merely syncategorematic; that is, that the truth connector . . . *is true* is not a predicate or a verb. Frege cannot draw such a conclusion, since he has no place for the syncategorematic in his logical symbolism.

Kahn's understanding of Epsilon 4 and Theta 10 as dealing with the two poles of truth-making correspondence needs to be rejected both on philosophical and exegetical grounds. However, the *apophantik* conception allows us to identify a shift in topic from Epsilon 4 to Theta 10, namely, from judgments to facts, without any commitment to a correspondence theory of truth.

In light of the *apophantik* account of truth we can see that Theta 10 deals with the being of facts—namely, of combination *in reality*—while Epsilon 4 deals with the being true of combination and separation *in the soul*. Even though both are acts of the same syncategorematic capacity, the being of a fact is different from the being of a judgment. Let me mention two deep and related differences between facts and judgments. First, (p or not-p) is a tautology, but of course (A judges p or A judges not-p) is false when A does not hold any view as to whether or not p is the case. Therefore, the syncategorematic capacity p, which is active in reality as a positive or negative fact, may not necessarily be active in a soul as the judgment p or as the judgment not-p. The priority of facts to judgments noted by Aristotle in the opening of Theta 10 reflects this disanalogy: "For it is not because of our truly thinking you to be pale that you are pale, but it is rather because you are pale that we who say this speak the truth." That p holds, rather than not-p, is not explained by the fact that A believes p truly as opposed to believing not-p or believing p falsely; for p holds, even if A has no opinion as to whether it does or not.

Second, the syncategorematic capacity p is negatively active in the intellect as not-p, namely, through the (potential) use of the negation sign; but the world, by contrast to the soul / intellect, is not a language-user, and thus the negative act, separation, does not inhere in it by means of the negation sign. Thus a separation, i.e., a negative fact (e.g., that book is not red), sometimes holds in virtue of a combination (e.g., that book is blue) being the case, i.e., in virtue of a positive fact.

The second puzzle was the curious position of Theta 10 as the concluding chapter of a book devoted to the concepts of activity and capacity and the corresponding senses of being. Insofar as combination and separation are and are not acts of two-way capacities, the discussion of them in Theta 10 properly belongs both inside and outside of Theta. This explains its place at the end of the book.

A categorematic being is signified by a categorematic expression—namely, by an element of a simple predication. As such, a substance and its determinations are categorematic beings, and clearly capacities and the activities of those capacities are also categorematic insofar as they are determinations of substances. By contrast, positive and negative facts—combination and separation—are not categorematic, they can only be stated by a proposition, and cannot be signified by anything categorematic.

We can sharpen the point by ruling out another possible interpretation of combinations as categorematic. One of the central themes of book Theta is the distinction between two ways in which a subject can be predicatively determined: *in capacity,* and *in activity.* For example, an empty glass is full of water in capacity, but is empty in activity or actuality. The topics of Theta—the concepts of capacity and activity and the corresponding senses of being—are of course related, since one can say that a subject is some particular way in capacity in virtue of possessing a certain capacity (e.g., the glass is full in capacity in virtue of possessing the capacity to be filled).

We can also associate this difference between being in the sense of being-in-capacity and being in the sense of being-in-activity with a difference in assertoric force, namely, with different ways of predicating or saying something of something. Since all predicates can be predicated in capacity or in activity, the difference between being-in-capacity and being-in-activity can be described as *cross-categorematic*.

But the difference between the combination and the separation that make up a contradictory pair is not a difference between modes of predication—of saying that something is the case with respect to a subject. For saying or holding that something is not the case is not a special way of saying or holding that something is the case; negating a determination of a subject is not a special way of determining that subject. A contradictory difference is therefore not *cross-categorematic*. The difference between combination and separation is not a difference in the way that something can hold of something else.

The contradictory difference between simple combinations and separations is neither categorematic nor cross-categorematic. Instead, as we concluded, it is a syncategorematic difference. Consequently, a combination cosignified or stated by an affirmation is not a categorematic being.

Thus we can conclude that Theta 10 does not belong to the study of the categorematic senses of being that precedes Theta, nor does it belong to the study of the cross-categorematic senses of being that takes place in the previous chapters of Theta.

The third puzzle concerns the superlative *kuriôtata*, which Aristotle uses in Theta 10 for being in the sense of being-true.

In the opening of Theta 10 Aristotle presents three senses of being.[24] The first sense of being corresponds to the ten categories, substance being the principal category. The second sense is that of capacity and activity; predicates in each category can be said of the subject either in capacity or activity.

The third sense of being is being and non-being in the sense of combination and of separation; this sense is the syncategorematic sense of being.

I present this hierarchy of the senses of being in order to show that the syncategorematic sense of being as being-true, and non-being as being false, is in fact the dominant sense. For any categorematic being *to be* is precisely for it to partake in a combination. Of course, a substance and an accident of substance partake in combination in a different sense. A substance partakes

---

[24] In *Metaphysics* Delta 7 Aristotle distinguishes the senses of being *per accidens* from the sense of being *per se*. Being *per accidens* is set aside by Aristotle as parasitic on being *per se*, arguably because such being involves an explicit or implicit conjunction. The list in Theta 10 is of the senses of being *per se*.

in a combination by being its determinable subject, whereas an accident or a predicative determination partakes by actually combining—by being the form of the positive fact in question. Hence, categorematic beings of different categories are said *to be*[25] in different senses. A substance *is,* by partaking in combinations or separations, whereas an accident or a predicative determination of any category *is,* only by partaking in combination, i.e., in positive facts. This asymmetry between substance and other categories is invoked to show that substances are prior among categorematic beings. Since, for any categorematic being to be is for it to be *in* a syncategorematic combination, i.e., in a positive fact, being in the sense of being-true—syncategorematic being—is the dominant sense of being. This dominance should be understood together with the priority of substance among the categorematic beings as two aspects of one insight.[26]

---

[25] *To be* is used here as complete copula that expresses existence. I would suggest that this is the way to read Aristotle's use of the verb of being in the list of the different senses of being in Delta 7 or Theta 10.

[26] In the context of the discussion of being in sense of being-true in Theta 10, Aristotle proceeds from the discussion of truth and falsehood in terms of combination and separation to discuss another site of being-true which is neither combination nor separation: that of the simples, and the noetic grasp of the simples (*to asuntheta*). The simples are essences and divine beings. Aristotle describes the grasp of simples as touch or contact (*thigein*) which as such is immune to error or falsehood. This grasp is not something that can be negated, and as such is not judgment/assertion. This dense and enigmatic passage (1051b17–1052a4), which communicates with *De Anima* 3.6, may be the key to comprehending Aristotle's notion of first philosophy. Here, I will only make the brief observation that a simple, according to Aristotle, is a syncategormatic unity which, unlike a combination, is not paired with a separation. As a syncategorematic unity, a simple cannot be predicatively determined, and yet it is not itself a predicative determination. It may be thought-provoking to consider an analogy between simples and tautologies, for the latter are also purely syncategorematic sites of truth, the grasp of which is immune to error. Insofar as Aristotelian theology is concerned with such simples it lacks categorematic content, and therefore cannot be regarded as a special science—this may shed a light on why Aristotle identifies theology with first philosophy.

On the Quietism of the Stranger

1.

In his dialogue the *Sophist,* Plato stages a dramatic hunt, within discourse, for the Sophist. The Sophist is a con artist who successfully poses as one who is wise about all things by, for example, bewildering his audience with apparent demonstrations of shocking theses—which he creates by exploiting linguistic ambiguities—and by equivocating without any care for truth or meaningfulness.

The two who are embarked on the hunt are the Stranger: a nameless philosopher from Elea, and his young and virtuous Athenian assistant/interlocutor, Theaetetus. They aim to catch the Sophist by defining the nature of his activity. At the outset they are at a disadvantage, for their hands are tied by the authority of Parmenides of Elea, who had argued that all attempts to talk of what is not, and thus of illusion and falsity, result in empty or incoherent chatter.

The Stranger honors Parmenides with title "father Parmenides," presumably for being the founder of philosophy as the "logical" study of being and thinking. In order to prove themselves the true descendants of Parmenides, viz., as philosophers, and distinguish themselves from the Sophists who, arguably, are themselves the bastard offspring of Parmenides, the Sophist-hunters need to free themselves from Parmenides's paternal authority (ironically, they need to show that his arguments are somehow sophistic).

"Don't think I am turning this into some kind of parricide" (241d), the Stranger tells Theaetetus, before adding that "in order to defend ourselves we're going to subject father Parmenides' saying to further examination."

In the middle part of the dialogue, the Stranger is out to show, by removing the Parmenidean difficulties, that the talk of what is not and of falsity need not collapse into incoherent or empty chatter. These puzzles are arguments that appear to show that talk of what is not and falsity are necessarily nonsensical. After dealing constructively with difficulties concerning *negation,* he tells Theaetetus that a correct account of the simple *logos* (proposition / statement) is required in order to vindicate the talk of false *logoi* in the face of the Parmenidean ban on mixing being and non-being.

2.

The discussion in 261c6–262e2 can be described as *the revelation of the logos in philosophy.* In this passage the idea that a *logos* is the locus of truth and falsity in virtue of being articulated—that is, in virtue of having an internal structure—is introduced for the first time. The crucial insight here is that "saying something"—which is what the utterer of a simple proposition does—is different from merely naming; and that, due to this difference, saying something, by contrast to naming or mentioning something, can be true or false. To achieve this "saying something" the simplest *logos* must be composed of two parts that play different roles: a *name* that singles out something, i.e., the subject, and a *verb* which is associated with the act of saying something of or about the subject. Thus, the Stranger teaches that the minimal locus of truth and falsity in discourse must be a combination *(an interweaving)* of a name and a verb.

3.

As soon as the Stranger concludes his lesson about the elements of the *logos,* he invites Theaetetus to consider two simple propositions—"Theaetetus sits" and "Theaetetus flies"—and prompts him to concede that while the first is true and the second is false, neither proposition is about anyone but Theaetetus himself.

The Stranger then proposes some concise characterizations of what constitutes the truth and the falsehood of such propositions:

(I) The true one says of things that are about you that they are, while (263b4) (II) the false one says different things from the things that are (263b7); that is (III) it says, of things that are not, that they are (263b9).[1]

4.

The characterization of the falsehood of simple positive propositions in terms of *difference* in formula (II) is meant to show that a proposition can be coherently described as false if the Parmenidean difficulty regarding the intelligibility of "things that are not" in formula (III) is removed. But one wonders: What precisely is this difficulty that the Stranger is seeking here to remove by invoking the notion of *difference?*

Two recent interpretations give different answers to this question. The first, which I call the *analytical interpretation* (and of which there are several rival variants in the literature), proposes that the Stranger solves the Parmenidean puzzles and removes the difficulties through an analysis—a relational construal—of the truth and falsehood of simple judgments; this analysis is based on the segmentation of the *logos* into name and verb. John McDowell's dissenting interpretation, which we can title the *deflationary interpretation,* denies that the Stranger puts forward the characterization of the complexity of the *logos* as a basis for an analysis of truth or falsehood.[2] According to the deflationist reading, the Stranger does not aim to explain truth and falsehood by reference to the unity and complexity of the simple *logos,* but only means to show a puzzle or a philosophical difficulty concerning falsity can be removed by correcting a confusion about the actual use of the negation sign.

---

[1] I shall follow Lesley Brown's advice, and eliminate plural forms in these formulations, which she argues serve merely as a stylistic device. Brown supports this by observing that "Theaetetus sits," which plainly says one thing about Theaetetus, is described as saying *ta onta,* things that are. See Brown, "*The Sophist* on Statement, Predications and Falsehood," in *The Oxford Handbook of Plato,* ed. Gail Fine (Oxford: Oxford University Press, 2008).

[2] "Falsehood and Not-being in Plato's *Sophist,*" in *The Engaged Intellect.*

I shall try to show that, according to the Stranger, the notions of truth and falsity are to be understood together with, and as equally basic as, the notion of a combination of name and verb. The aim of the Stranger is to associate truth and falsity with this notion of combination, rather than to offer an analysis which explains the truth aptness of the *logos* in term of a combination and its elements. So while both analytical and deflationist interpretations misunderstand the Stranger's lesson, each of them get some aspect of it right.

4.1.

From the perspective of the analytical interpretation, the Stranger should appear familiar to us. We should, for example, recognize the difficulty concerning falsehood with which he struggles, for this difficulty, which McDowell dubs the *deep puzzle,* is none other than the one that Wittgenstein expresses in the following question:

> How can one think what is not the case? If I think King's College is on fire when it is not, the fact of its being on fire does not exist. Then how can I think it?[3]

This puzzle arises from the following reasoning: Whereas a true judgment/proposition judges/says what is the case, a false one judges/says what is not (the case)—but what is not does not exist; it is nothing, hence a false judgment/proposition judges/says nothing and is therefore not a judgment/proposition at all.

The deep puzzle arises, McDowell notes, once the truth and falsehood of propositions are construed in terms of *states of affairs,* veridical beings that McDowell describes as

> a chunk of reality with a structure such as to mirror that of the proposition or statement it would render true.[4]

---

[3] Wittgenstein, *The Blue and Brown Books,* 31.

[4] "Falsehood and Not-being in Plato's *Sophist,*" 19. This description suggests a conception of states of affairs as senses of true propositions, which McDowell endorses in his later work. See, for example, the discussion of facts in "Evans's Frege," *The Engaged Intellect,* 169.

Insofar as the puzzle arises from this notion of a state of affairs, one can also say that it arises from the veridical use of the copula as Kahn understands it, namely, with the application of *. . . is the case* to a propositional complex.[5] McDowell assumes, with Kahn, that a veridical being—a state of affairs—is a propositionally structured complex whose intrinsic being is separable from its veridical being or non-being. *Pace* Kahn, he argues that since the introduction of such a notion was a modern development, the imputation of the idea of states of affairs to the Greeks must be anachronistic. But this charge of anachronism reveals the inadequacy of McDowell's contemporary conception of veridical beings—one that dissociates the intrinsic propositional unity of a veridical being from its veridical being or non-being.

McDowell argues that Plato's new discovery of the segmentation of the simple *logos* does not yet provide him with this notion of a *state of affairs,* and that since anyway one cannot find this notion in the *Sophist,* the deep puzzle cannot be the one that worries him.[6]

The *deep puzzle* concerning falsehood ("How can I think what is not the case?") appears to be closely associated with another puzzle, which the young Wittgenstein described as *the mystery of negation:*

---

[5] See Kahn, "The Greek Verb 'To Be,' and the Concept of Being."

[6] McDowell distinguishes between three puzzles concerning falsehood in his reading of the *Sophist:*

(1) The deep puzzle, which according to McDowell is not addressed in the *Sophist.*

(2) The puzzle which the Stranger is in fact addressing and removing.

(3) A collection of puzzles that were in the air at Plato's time which, without being directly addressed, are removed by the very characterization of the *logos* as structured (i.e., by the distinction between naming and saying). These puzzles arise for a philosophical account of language that is indifferent to, or ignorant of, the distinction between mentioning and saying. McDowell dubs such an account, which is comes up in different places in Plato and Aristotle, the *crude position.*

The crude position gives the appearance that it is impossible for one person to contradict another person or herself, since all one can achieve by speech is changing the subject matter. The distinction between naming and saying is precisely what is needed to render the possibility of contradiction unproblematic by dissolving this appearance.

As for (2)—the puzzle concerning falsehood that the Stranger addresses directly— McDowell takes it to be an instance of the puzzle concerning negation that the Stranger removes.

It is the mystery of negation: This is not how things are and yet we can say *how* things are *not.*[7]

The mystery resides in the fact that, by using the negation sign, I can be right in saying something even though what I say is not (the case)—is nothing. This is a challenge to the very intelligibility of the notion of the truth of a negative claim. This puzzle, like the deep puzzle, arises from understanding truth in terms of the existence of states of affairs, and so according to the deflationist reading it cannot be the puzzle that the Stranger is addressing in the *Sophist*. We shall see that, according to the analytical interpretation, the Stranger indirectly resolves this puzzle through a semantic analysis of negative predicates.

4.2.

If it is the case that when a predicative proposition is true its contradictory counterpart must be false, then these two puzzles are identical; for the falsity-conditions of a positive predicative proposition are the same as the truth-conditions of its negative counterpart. This sameness of the deep puzzle and the mystery of negation points toward the larger philosophical task of attaining a view of propositional complexity from which the following four syllogisms of thinking and being will be revealed together, in one glance, as valid and complete—that is, as requiring no extra premises.

A.
  1. A judges p
  2. p
  3. A truly judges p
B.
  1. A judges p
  2. not-p
  3. A falsely judges p
C.
  1. A judges not-p
  2. not-p
  3. A truly judges not-p

[7] Wittgenstein, *Notebooks 1914–1916,* 30.

D.
   1. A judges not-p
   2. p
   3. A falsely judges not-p

I shall refer to A and C as the negative and positive *truth-maker* syllogisms of thinking and being; I will refer to B and D as the negative and positive *false-maker* syllogisms. This perspective should reveal that, in holding the premises of any of these inferences to be true, a thinker is already holding the conclusion to be true.

The deep puzzle and the mystery of negation show that we still lack a proper account of propositional complexity—one that elucidates the dependence of thinking on being (on reality, the world). Certainly one will not find such a conception in the recent philosophical literature. The widely accepted Fregean framework, for example, is unable to capture the logical unity of the above syllogisms, since they all involve the occurrence of the same expression, "p," both inside and outside the context of indirect discourse. The former is an intensional context, and thus, according to Frege, one in which the expression occurs with a different signification.[8] Hence, from a Fregean point of view, the premises of these syllogisms are logically unconnected. Yet to recognize these syllogisms as self-evident, one must recognize that the conclusion reveals the logical unity of the premises.

Donald Davidson advanced a "semantically innocent" account of the logical form of indirect discourse—that is, an account according to which expressions signify in the same way both inside and outside of intensional contexts—that sought to respect extensionalism. However, it can be shown, first of all, that this account fails to display the contradictory unity of the pair <A judges p, A judges not-p> and, secondly, that it fails to reveal the logical connection between the premises in the syllogisms.[9]

---

[8] The Fregean's deflationary construal of the conclusions as conjunctions of the premises offers only the illusion of an account, since it assumes that the complex signified by "p" in intensional contexts has the same truth-value as the assertion "p."

[9] An account of indirect discourse is semantically innocent if it recognizes p as having the same significance when it stands by itself to express a judgment in direct discourse, as when it is employed in the context of indirect discourse: A says p. The Fregean account of indirect discourse lacks such innocence. Davidson's account of indirect discourse

I will try to show in this chapter that the treasure we seek is contained in Plato's *Sophist*. We shall find in the dialogue the material needed to overcome the various philosophical obstacles that preclude us from seeing that the syllogisms of thinking and being are self-evident.

5.

(I) The true one says of a thing that is about you that it is (263b4).

According to the analytical interpretation, (I) is an account of the truth of a positive predicative proposition, in terms of a relation that holds between the significations of its subject and predicate components.

The "thing" mentioned in (I) is an *attribute* (the philosophical terms *property, kind, universal, property, form* could all be used instead here) understood as a being *(on)* that is *signified* or *expressed by* the predicate, i.e., by the verb of the proposition. Thus, on the analytical interpretation, (I) is a definition of the existence of a state of affairs, and thus of the truth of the simple positive proposition in terms of the relation: . . . *is the case with respect to* . . . that holds between an attribute and a particular. For example, the truth of

---

purports to be semantically innocent by denying that p is a semantic or even a syntactic component of A says p.

Davidson provides the following description of his account as applied to the indirect speech report "Galileo said that the Earth moves":

> The paratactic semantic approach to indirect discourse tells us to view an utterance of 'Galileo said that the Earth moves' as consisting of the utterance of two sentences, "Galileo said that" and "The Earth moves." The "that" refers to the second utterance, and the first utterance is true if and only if an utterance of Galileo's was the same in content as ("translates") the utterance to which the "that" refers. (Davidson 1979: 39 / 1984: 176–177)

Thus, according to this account, what appears as a subordinate clause in indirect speech is not really a logical part or element of the speech at all, but instead a worldly item to which the demonstrative singular term that allegedly occurs in the report refers. As such, these clauses cannot participate in the logical form of the inferences in which the reports occur. In particular, Davidson's account of indirect speech renders unintelligible the validity of the syllogisms of saying and being of the form:
(I) A said p, p, hence, A truly said p. (II) A said p, *not-p* hence, A falsely said p, unintelligible.

Theaetetus is sitting consists in the attribute *sitting* standing in the relation of 'being the case with respect to' *Theaetetus,* namely, the existence of the state of affairs that Theaetetus is sitting. On this construal of states of affairs, a simple positive judgment / assertion is understood through the relation between the judging subject, an attribute which is what is said, and a particular about which the attribute is said.

If the truth of a judgment / proposition consists in the existence of a state of affairs, which in turn is understood as the obtaining of the relation . . . *is the case with respect to . . . ,* the falsehood of a simple judgment / proposition, understood as the nonexistence of such a state of affairs, consequently consists in the nonobtaining of the relation in question.

It therefore transpires that the relational construal of positive judgments, and the existence of a state of affairs, allows us to specify a nonexistent state of affairs, and to ascribe a false positive judgment, by mentioning a particular and an attribute which do exist—independently of whether or not the attribute is or is not the case with respect to the particular.

The attempt to define the absence of a fact as the nonobtaining of a relation between a particular and an attribute faces a further Eleatic obstacle, for the notion of "not being the case with respect to . . ." is vulnerable to Parmenidean worries about the intelligibility of negation. For example, if we say that the falsehood of *Theaetetus flies* consists in *flying* not being the case concerning *Theaetetus,* we encounter the mystery of negation as described above (as well as a puzzle concerning the determinate content of negative predicates, which I shall discuss below).

Now, according to the analytical interpretation, the Stranger's invocation of *difference* purports to overcome this further obstacle, which is created by the use of the idiom "things that are not" in formula (III). According to the analytical interpretation, difference is a relation between attributes, i.e., those entities signified by predicates. The analytical interpreter reads (II) as "the false says of something different that it is the case concerning you," i.e., as a characterization of falsity in terms of the relation between attributes.

The falsehood of a positive predicative proposition consists in its saying something about the subject which is different from what is the case about the subject. This account of falsehood is not meant to be understood simply in terms of the nonidentity of two attributes—one of which is said of the subject, and one of which is the case with respect to the subject—since it is evident that there are many things that are the case with respect to Theaetetus and which differ from *sitting* (e.g., *listening*), even when it is the case that Theaetetus is sitting.

Thus, the disagreement between rival analytical interpretations of (II) turns on the different ways of interpreting *difference* as a relation that holds between attributes. The two main variants are the so-called *Oxford interpretation,* and the *incompatible range interpretation.* On the Oxford interpretation, the falsity of the proposition *Theaetetus flies* is constituted by *flying* being different from anything that is the case concerning Theaetetus. According to this reading, the relation of *difference,* is simply the nonidentity between attributes, and it holds that a universal quantifier ranging over attributes is implicit in (II).

According to the incompatible range interpretation, *Theaetetus flies* is false because *flying* is different from an attribute taken from a range or family of attributes that are incompatible with *flying* (e.g., *sitting*) and that apply to Theaetetus. The relation of *difference* holds between different attributes within a family of incompatible attributes, and an existential quantifier is said to be implicit in (II).[10] Thus, whichever way one understands *difference,* on the analytical interpretation the Stranger successfully shows that talk of the *nonexistence of a state of affairs or the absence of fact* can be vindicated without having to conjure up any irreducible nonexistent propositional unities or states of affairs.

---

[10] The analytical interpretations of truth and falsehood deal with the truth and falsehood of positive judgments. They are incomplete, therefore, insofar as it is unclear how they can be extended in order to account for the truth and falsehood of negative judgments. McDowell points out that, in an early section of the dialogue, the Stranger gives a disjunctive definition of the falsehood of positive and negative judgment: False saying is (i) saying what is not is or (ii) saying what is not (240e–241a). The first part covers the false positive judgment "Theaetetus flies," whereas the second part covers the false negative judgment "Theaetetus is not sitting." As McDowell stresses, since the analytical interpretation addresses only one half of this definition, it cannot be right about which difficulty the Stranger is struggling with.

6.

Suppose that the analytical interpretation gets it right—that the Sophist is trying to escape by invoking the deep puzzle, and that the Stranger's response is an analysis of truth and falsehood that diffuses the deep puzzle. If so, McDowell wants to assure the Sophist that he is in no danger of being caught, that he can brush off the attempt to define him with the following rebuttal:

> Attributes, like in *flight,* are not the sort of thing that I thought a description of falsehood in beliefs and statements would have to represent as not being. And it was not in the sense you exploit—not being in relation to something—but in precisely the sense you agree is problematic—not being anything at all—that I thought a description of falsehood would have to represent my different items, situations or states of affairs, as not being. You have not shown that the description of falsehood I found problematic is not compulsory, dictated by the nature of the concept of falsehood; and you have certainly not shown it is not problematic.[11]

The falsehood of "Theaetetus is in flight" consists, McDowell insists, precisely in the fact that the state of affairs that the proposition represents—or perhaps the flight that someone uttering the proposition would be accusing *Theaetetus* of being engaged—is nothing at all. As such, the deep puzzle cannot be removed by understanding falsehood as the absence of a fact, or the nonexistence of a state of affairs, if that means the failure of a relation to hold between beings that exist independently of whether the judgment is true or false.

We can understand the grounds of McDowell's critique of the relational conception of the existence of states of affairs, and consequently his rejection of the analytical interpretation, by recalling Wittgenstein's criticism of Russell's multiple relation theory of judgment. For, as we shall see, Russell's account essentially agrees with the account of judgment and truth that the analytical interpretation ascribes to the Stranger.

[11] McDowell, "Falsehood and Not-being in Plato's *Sophist*," 16.

6.1. Russell on Propositions and Judgment

Russell adopted the multiple relation theory of judgment in 1910, after giving up on the doctrine of propositions that he unsuccessfully tried to develop in his *Principles of Mathematics*. The earlier doctrine held that judgment is a relation between a judging subject and a proposition: a nonlinguistic, non-mental entity that is semantically self-contained, in the sense that its truth-value depends only on its intrinsic character.[12]

Russell describes the problem that forced him to abandon this earlier doctrine as follows:

> If we allow that all judgments have Objectives, we shall have to allow that there are judgments which are false. Thus there will be in the world entities, not dependent upon the existence of judgments, which can be described as objective falsehoods. This is in itself almost incredible: we feel that there could be no falsehoods if there were no minds to make mistakes. But it has the further drawback that it leaves the difference between truth and falsehood quite inexplicable. ("On the Nature of Truth and Falsehood," in *The Collected Papers of Bertrand Russell*, vol. 6, *Logic and Philosophical Papers 1909–1913*, ed. J. G. Slater [London: Allen and Unwin, 1992], 119)

By taking propositions to be semantically self-contained, Russell was committed to thinking that falsehood was immanent to propositions, that thus to real beings, a consequence that he later considered to be incredible. But the stronger charge against the doctrine of propositions is that the understanding of propositional unity as immanent to the proposition, external to the mind, and intrinsically true or false, results in rendering falsity and negation unintelligible. It also has the absurd consequence to understand a proposition is to know its truth-value. Russell concluded that the difficulty concerning falsehood can be avoided by rejecting the doctrine of proposi-

---

[12] According to this earlier doctrine, the semantical self-containedness of propositions implies that neither a proposition nor its constituents are semantically related to beings that are external to the proposition. Russell refers to the constituents of propositions as *terms*. The unity of the proposition is independent of the judging mind, which is external to it, and the difference between propositions and mere aggregates of propositional constituents, i.e., terms, lies, according to Russell, in the role of the verb in the proposition, which actively binds the proposition together.

tions with its assumption of immanent falsity, in favor of a multiple relation theory of judgment admitting only facts, i.e., existing states of affairs.

On the 1910 version of the theory, when Cassio judges that Desdemona loves Othello, a four-place relation of judging holds between Cassio, Desdemona, loving, and Othello, respectively. On the old analysis, this judgment was ascribed by a sentence of the form "J(x,p)." Now it is ascribed by a sentence of the form "J(x,a,R,b)." Cassio's judgment is true, for there exists a corresponding fact: Desdemona's loving Othello. Russell conceives of this fact in the same way that he earlier thought of propositions: as a complex united by the governing verb. Cassio's judgment therefore consists of the four-place judging relation that holds between Cassio, Desdemona, loving, and Othello. Through this analysis of judgment, Russell eliminates false complexes from his ontology. There is, for example, no longer a false complex in which the relation of loving joins Desdemona to Cassio. Truth thus consists in the existence of a state of affairs corresponding to a judgment-fact; and the absence of a corresponding fact falsifies Othello's judgment that Desdemona loves Cassio.

The stumbling block Russell encountered in developing this took the form of difficulties concerning falsehood and negation (and more generally, compound propositions). The being, i.e., existence, of a proposition "Desdemona loves Cassio" is constituted by "love" holding between Desdemona and Cassio; but it seems therefore to follow that the mere existence of the proposition renders it true, and consequently that false propositions and false judgments are unintelligible.

One can try to escape this consequence by allowing that a term can occur as a verb in two ways: positively or negatively, namely, as a nexus of truth or as a nexus of falsehood. But this clashes with Russell's treatment of compound propositions. According to Russell the subordinate components of a compound proposition are terms in it, but a proposition which is constituted by a verb cannot occur as a term in another proposition or propositions. Using the terminology that we introduced earlier, we can say that, for Russell, the logical connectives are categorematic, i.e., relational, whereas propositions constituted by an active verb are syncategorematic. Russell tries to solve the problem by allowing a proposition to occur both as a proposition, i.e., *asserted,* and as a term in a compound, i.e., *unasserted.* But since, according to Russell (*pace* Frege), force is immanent or internal to the proposition, it is not clear how such a view can make sense of the logical relation between p and not-p, since the embedded "p" in not-p is different than p. In other words, this doctrine fails to respect Frege's point. Moreover, if the verb in asserted propositions can occur positively or negatively, then the unasserted proposition can be associated with either, and so is indeterminate between being unasserted p or being unasserted not-p.

Russell's examples are relational propositions, but this is not essential to the theory. We shall limit our discussion to the theory's treatment of simple nonrelational judgments.[13] For example, Socrates's judgment that *Theaetetus is sitting* can be ascribed to Socrates, according to the multiple relation theory, by a proposition of the form J(Socrates, Theaetetus, sitting). This theory purports to provide us with an analysis of the ascription of the judgment / assertion that *Theaetetus is sitting* as an open proposition, J(x, Theaetetus, sitting), that can be ascribed to thinkers or speakers.

The truth of the judgment consists in the existence of the state of affairs that Theaetetus is sitting, and thus in the attribute "sitting" being the case with respect to Theaetetus. The falsehood of the judgment J(Socrates, Theaetetus, flying) consists in the absence of a corresponding relational fact. It is clear that this analysis of positive judgment agrees with the account of positive judgment that the analytical interpretations ascribe to the Stranger.

In 1913–1914 Wittgenstein advanced some objections to this account of judgment which Russell came to recognize were devastating. The core of Wittgenstein's criticism appears in the *Notes on Logic*:

> When we say A judges that, etc., then we have to mention a whole proposition which A judges. It will not do to mention only its constituents, or its constituents and form but not in the proper order. This shows that a proposition itself must occur in the statement to the effect that it is judged. For instance, however "not-p" may be explained, the question "What is negated?" must have a meaning. (96)

The point concerning negation at the end of the passage is a requirement on the explicit logical rendition of negation. This requirement is presented as an instance of the general requirement that applies also to the analysis of indirect discourse. Thus, the occurrence of the proposition "*p*" within indirect discourse, e.g., "A judges that *p*," is treated, in this passage, on a par with the occurrence of the proposition "*p*" in the complex proposition "not-*p*." This will of course seem strange to contemporary philosophers, who are accustomed to drawing a distinction between the occurrence of a proposition

---

[13] Hence, we shall ignore the special problems that symmetrical relations pose to the *multiple relation theory of judgment*.

in an extensional truth-functional context (e.g., "p" in "not-p") and in an intensional context (e.g., "p" in "A believes that p"). I shall propose later that assimilating the issues of the context of negation and the context of indirect discourse lies at the heart of Plato's clarification of negation in the face of the Parmenidean difficulties.

In order to satisfy the requirement that the question "What is negated?" has a meaning, a relational construal of "not-p" must reveal its contradictory unity with "p"; that is, it should reveal, without any reference to further premises, that "not-p" is the contradictory of "p." But it is easy to see that, by not allowing positive predication to occur within the negative predication, the relational construal fails to display the unity of a contradictory pair of simple judgments.

Whether the multiple relation construal of *Theaetetus is not sitting* has the form J*(x, Theaetetus, sitting), in which J*(x, . . . , __) ascribes a negative judgment to x, or the form J(x, Theaetetus, not-Sitting), in which not-Sitting is a negative attribute, the contradictory unity with the positive judgment is lost. The immediate logical unity of contradictory judgments, one which is displayed by the repetition of the same propositional sign "p" inside and outside the negated proposition, is lost in a relational construal of propositions. As such it fails to capture the logical identity of the propositions it tries to render. I take this to be the point that Wittgenstein was bringing to Russell's attention.

We can now apply this lesson to the case of indirect discourse. Consider the claim "A judges that *Theaetetus is sitting.*" A construal of the logical form of this claim ought to reveal the validity and completeness of the positive truth-maker and falsity-maker inferences, namely, of the following inferences:

(1) S judges that Theaetetus is sitting, and (2) Theaetetus is sitting, hence (3) S truly judges that Theaetetus is sitting, and from (1*) S judges Theaetetus is flying, (2*) Theaetetus is not flying, hence (3*) S falsely judges that Theaetetus is flying.

But now, since (1) is rendered by a relational analysis as J(x, J(S, Theaetetus, Sitting)) and (2) as J(x, Theaetetus, Sitting), it is clear that this analysis cannot capture the validity and completeness of these inferences. It is by the repetition of a repeatable "p" within and without the context of indirect discourse, i.e., in (1) and (2) and in (1*) and (2*), that the validity and completeness of these inferences are displayed and secured.

On another occasion Wittgenstein presents the same criticism of the multiple relational analysis of judgment in a slightly different form:

> I can now express my objections to your theory of judgments exactly: I believe it is obvious that, from the prop[osition] "A judges that (say) a is in the Rel[ation] R to b," if correctly analyzed, the proposition "aRb or ~aRb" must follow directly without the use of any premises. (Letter to Russell, 1913, in *Wittgenstein in Cambridge: Letters and Documents 1911–1951* [Oxford: Blackwell, 2008], 29)

The requirement here is that "A thinks p" will reveal its direct internal connection to the proposition p, namely, the judgment/assertion I ascribe to A must be logically connected to the judgment/assertion that I can make myself (a capacity expressible by the tautology "p or not-p"). Given a relational or Fregean construal of the logical form of "A thinks p," this immediate logical unity between the ascription of judgment to another, and an assertion that one can oneself make, is lost. The unity, however, is displayed by the repetition of the propositional letter p. The crux of Wittgenstein's criticism is that Russell's construal of judgment cannot acknowledge Frege's observation that the same proposition can occur asserted and unasserted.

6.2. "Don't think I am turning this into some kind of parricide" (*Sophist* 241d).

In a letter to a friend in 1916, Russell describes the devastating effect that Wittgenstein's criticism had on him some years earlier:

> His criticism, though I don't think you realized it at the time, was an event of first-rate importance in my life, and affected everything that I have done since. I saw he was right, and saw that I could not hope ever again to do fundamental work in philosophy. (*The Autobiography of Bertrand Russell: 1914–1944* [London: Allen and Unwin, 1968], 57)

But Wittgenstein's criticism of the relational analysis of judgment did not stop other philosophers from continuing to attempt fundamental work in philosophy. Russell's multiple relation theory of judgment can be seen as an attempt to resolve the deep puzzle and the mystery of negation, such that its failure appears to leave us with these difficulties—and yet contemporary philosophers seem untroubled by them. We can therefore ask whether they see a way out of the difficulties to which Russell was blind.

I take it that the answer is that the relational construal which surfaced here in the analytical interpretations of the *Sophist* was generally rejected in favor of a Fregean account of thoughts as the senses of propositions. According to this account, p has no intrinsic association with assertoric force and is therefore semantically autonomous relative to not-p. This account recognizes p as the same in (i) "p" and (ii) "not-p," but denies that p is the same in (i) and in (iii) "A judges that p."

It is clear then that the Fregean account is not what Wittgenstein was seeking when he wrote to Russell to express sympathy with his predicament:

> I am very sorry to hear that my objection to your theory of judgment paralyses you. I think it can only be removed by a correct theory of propositions. (22 July 1913, in *Wittgenstein in Cambridge: Letters and Documents 1911–1951*, 42)

Nonetheless, since the Fregean account subscribes to Frege's point, it can appear to be safe from Wittgenstein's criticism in the case of negation.

6.3.

There is a deep difference between Russell's propositions and Frege's thoughts: Russell's propositions have an immanent truth-value, whereas Frege's thoughts are immanently truth-valueless—their being true or false depends on something external to them. (I restrict the discussion here to simple, i.e., atomic, thoughts; for Frege, compound thoughts can be logically true or false, and thus, in a sense, have their truth-value intrinsically.) In other words, whereas veridical being or non-being is not extrinsic to a Russellian proposition it is extrinsic to the Fregean thought.

Russell distinguishes psychological and non-psychological senses of assertoric force. A judgment is construed as a psychological attitude toward a proposition; but semantical self-containedness, which is the fundamental assumption of Russell's doctrine of propositions, led him to say that a proposition contains an assertion in a non-psychological sense. We saw that this position faces insurmountable Parmenedian objections. There is an analogous distinction between psychological and logical notions of judgment in

Frege's system. The former notion is that of judgment as expressed by a predicate that is employed in indirect discourse to describe an attitude toward a thought; the second notion is that of judgment as manifested by the assertoric form of a sentence within direct discourse.

According to Frege, force in the logical sense is extrinsic to the primary locus of truth and falsity inside a propositional sign or judgment. Frege insists that this externality does not point to any larger propositional sign or to a larger content to which the force is internal; we can therefore say that the externality of force to the primary locus of truth and falsity is merely syncategorematic.

Frege is led by his conception of logical complexity to distinguish between the extensional identity of a propositional component, associated with its reference, from its logical or intensional identity that is associated with its sense. In Frege's system, the logical identity of a simple proposition, along with its sense, is independent of its truth-value. Fregean thoughts do not have immanent truth-values since their truth-value depends on the extension of the predicate, which is external to the identity of the thought.

If we presuppose the Fregean notion of *thought,* we can coherently describe thinkers as understanding propositions without having to know their truth-value; we can ascribe judgments with a certain thought as its content, even when this thought is false; and we can describe negation as a content modifier, that is, as part of the functional composition. Thus, it appears that the notion of a forceless truth- / falsity-bearer, something which is not intrinsically true or false, is precisely what is needed in order to put to rest all of philosophy's Parmenidean concerns.

It is not surprising therefore that philosophers may feel that they are saved from such anxieties by Frege's discoveries—specifically by the notion of a forceless truth-bearer which lacks an immanent truth-value. Indeed, within this widely accepted framework, the Parmenidean difficulties concerning falsehood and negation appear obsolete.

It is a direct consequence of Frege's view of the complexity of judgment and the propositional sign that the notion of *truth* bifurcates into, on the one hand, a value of functionally complex truth-bearers which are functionally determined by the references of their components and, on the other hand, the mark of success in judgment.

Through examining this bifurcation of the notion of truth I will try to show that Frege's conception of thoughts as forceless truth-bearers only provides an illusion of safety in the face of the Parmenidean difficulties, and that in fact it fails to provide an understanding of the proposition which allows us to do fundamental work in philosophy.

6.4. Frege on Truth

In Frege's writings *truth* (or *falsity*) is said in three different ways: first, we find truth in the sense of a concept: the *truth-predicate* ". . . is true," a first-order concept-expression which has the same syntactic character as a monadic logical connective such as negation. Second, there is truth in the sense of an object: the *True* as the truth-value to which propositions refer and which differs from the second truth-value: the *False*. Finally, there is truth in the sense that is associated with force. This is truth thought of as the essential moment of a successful judgment / assertion—the particular goal to which judgment, as a goal-directed act, is oriented.

Whereas *truth* in the third sense pertains to the act of judgment, *truth* in the first two senses pertains primarily to the forceless component of judgments and assertions, i.e., to thoughts and propositions. Truth and falsity, in these senses, are associated with linguistic expressions: namely, with the predicates " . . . is true" and " . . . is false"; and with the singular terms *True* and *False* that are the reference of propositions. It is a consequence of Frege's point that judgment / assertion cannot be identified with the application of a predicate, in particular not with the application of a truth-predicate. Hence, truth in the sense related to force cannot be identified with the use of a truth-predicate, and in fact cannot be manifested by any particular expression, but is instead associated with the assertoric form of propositions.

Within the *Begriffsschrift* the role of the truth-predicate is played by the content-stroke, i.e., the horizontal, which is a concept-word that has only the truth-value the *True* in its extension. The assertoric form of a proposition is associated with the judgment-stroke, in a way that manifests the internal difference, within a propositional sign, between its content-relevant features (i.e., its functional composition) and the assertoric form of a proposition (see Chapter 1 for a discussion of these). The truth-values the *True* and the *False* can be named by the identities 1 = 1, and 1 = 2, respectively.

The truth predicate cannot be senseless, since propositions in which it occurs are meaningful. Frege concluded that, since asserting "*p*" is the same as asserting "*p* is true," the truth-predicate is sense-transparent, namely, the sense of "*p is true*" is the same as the sense of "*p.*" Frege takes this to mean that the truth-predicate does not express a property of thought.

The truth-value which is signified by a proposition is determined relative to its composition by the reference of the components. The propositions with which we are concerned in our discussion are simple contingent propositions, e.g., Socrates is wise, and the truth-value of such propositions depends on the extension of the predicates in them. That these extensions are independent of the logical identity of the predicate is shown by the fact that we can understand a predicative thought without knowing its truth-value.

Here lies the deep difference between Russell's propositions and Frege's thoughts. Russell's propositions are semantically self-contained; the truth-value of a proposition depends only on the components and their unity in the proposition. Such a conception leaves no place for the semantic duality of sense and reference. By contrast, for Frege, the (nonlogical) truth of a thought depends on something which is not logically contained within it, and this dependence cannot be understood in terms of the relations between senses or thoughts. For example, since truth does not depend on sense, truth cannot be construed as a relational property of thought. We saw that Russell's conception of propositions as semantically self-contained breaks down in the face of false judgments. By making truth and falsity extrinsic to propositions or thoughts, Frege's conception promises to avoid the Parmenidean puzzles.

Frege glosses judging as *acknowledging* a thought to be true—but he warns the reader that this is not a definition, since the unity of content and act in judgment cannot be defined. Furthermore, he claims that the acknowledgment of a thought as being true cannot be construed as a transition from one thought to another, something he emphasizes in "On Sense and Reference":

> But combining subject and predicate, one reaches only a thought, never passes from sense to its *Bedeutung,* never from a thought to its truth-value. One moves at the same level but never advances from one level to the next. (*The Frege Reader*, 158)

Therefore *acknowledgment* cannot be construed as predication. Instead, Frege glosses it as a transition from a *thought* to the truth-value, the *True*;

thus, he explains judgment through the association of truth, in the sense related to force, and the *True*, in the sense of an object (the object which is signified by, e.g., $2 = 1 + 1$).

But this attempt to unify the truth of the judgment with the reference of its forceless content rests, I want to show, on an illusion.

Consider for example the simple judgment ⊢ *Pa*. The truth value of this judgment is identified by Frege with the reference of the forceless expression *Pa*.

Pa signifies truth if and only if *a* belongs to the extension of P, and therefore the truth-conditions for the judgment displayed by this proposition ⊢ *Pa* are specifiable by mentioning the extension determined by Px and *a*.

Frege describes the unity of *Pa* as that of the saturation of the unsaturated first-order functional expression by the argument expression. This saturation is not a relation between two relata, and thus unity of the proposition cannot be associated with a relation. Instead saturation must be described as a formal relation or as a nonrelational nexus. Thus, the simple proposition *Pa* cannot be specified by propositional components which are identifiable below the level, as it were, of propositional unity. Yet, the externality of the truth-value of the proposition means that the truth-condition of *Pa*, namely, the condition under which it refers to the *True*, is the obtaining of a truth-making relation on the level of reference, i.e., the inclusion of the object a under the extension determined by the predicate P. Of course, this truth-making relation is not by itself the reference of the proposition, whose only reference is its truth-value. But the differences between truth-values are associated with the obtaining and nonobtaining of such truth-making relations, which are associated with the formal relation of saturation.

But now one can ask: in virtue of what is the forceless combination *Pa* associated with the truth-making relation that *a* falls under the extension of P, and thus with the claim *Pa*, rather than with the truth-making relation that *a* does *not* fall under P (or falls under the extension of -*P*), and thus with the opposite claim -*Pa*? This question cannot be answered, since *Pa* does not display an assertion, and therefore there is nothing that associates it with the positive rather than the negative judgment. The association of the proposition *Pa*, conceived as forceless, with one of these conditions as its truth-making relation, understood in terms of the object the *True* rather than the other, smuggles assertoric force back into the predicative composition

Pa—force which Frege denies is there.[14] (Indeed, the very idea of *"something falling in the extension of a predicate,"* e.g., *wise,* must be associated with syncategorematic *directionality* in the sense introduced in Chapter 2, and thus with force.)

However, insofar as we deny that Frege's notion of forceless judgments is adequate, we once again find ourselves in Russell's predicament, at the very point at which he decided that he could no longer continue to do fundamental work in philosophy.

7. Negation

What puzzle or difficulty is the Stranger addressing in the discussion which concludes with the announcement (258b6–7) that the notion of "what is not" has been vindicated—the notion through which the elusive Sophist can finally be trapped? This discussion preceded the discussion of falsehood and the lesson of the *logos.*

The different interpretations agree that the difficulty addressed in this discussion has to do with the sense of negated predicates. Mourelatos glosses this difficulty, which he sees as lying at the center of Parmenides's *Poem,* by invoking a Homeric figure:

> In Homer the sea is called "boundless" precisely because it is unstructured, and because it lies outside islands (which are bounded) and beyond shores (which are boundaries). This Homeric contrast of the island against the *pontos apeiron,* "boundless sea," may well count as aptly as the Parmenidean image of the contrast between what-is and what-is-not. ("Some Alternatives in Interpreting Parmenides," 359)

Whereas in positive predications the subject is placed on a determinate, circumscribed island in logical space, negative predication launches the subject onto the boundless sea, and thus apparently does not determinate it in any way. From the perspective of the analytic interpretation, the challenge

---

[14] Wittgenstein presents a similar criticism of Frege's conception of truth in proposition 4.063 of the *Tractatus,* and ends his critique with the following conclusion: "The verb of the proposition is not 'is true' or 'is false' as Frege thought—but that which 'is true' must already contain the verb."

created by this difficulty is to specify the sense, i.e., the meaning, of the negative predicate without invoking negation.

At this point it is worth recalling an exegetical problem which readers of Plato are faced with when dealing with the meaning of negative predicates. In the *Sophist*, Plato seems to hold that removing the Parmenidean puzzle allows us to conclude that the negated predicate is associated with a determinate being. The Stranger says:

> Well then according to this account, is *the beautiful* more a being than *the not beautiful?*

Theaetetus responds:

> Not at all.

But this position appears to contradict Plato's clear rejection of negative kinds in the *Statesman*:

> One should make the division as most people in this country do; they separate the Hellenic race from all the rest as one, and to all the other races, which are countless in number and have no relation in blood or language to one another, they give the single name "barbarian"; then, because of this single name, they think it is a single kind. (262d)

Further on, I will propose a reading of Plato that explains why this is only an apparent contradiction.

7.1.

We have encountered two puzzles concerning negation: first, the mystery of negation, and second, the puzzle concerning the sense of negated predicates.

According to the analytical interpretation, the Stranger removes the two puzzles together by construing the sense of a negative predicate in terms of the relation of *difference* between attributes; whereas, according to the deflationary interpretation, the Stranger addresses only the second puzzle, and removes it by identifying the "grammatical" confusion which gives rise to the appearance of a difficulty here.

Both interpretations agree that the crucial move that enables the removal of the puzzle concerning negation occurs in passage 257b1–c4 (which follows the discussion of the communion of forms, and difference as a distinction between kinds).

8.

In the following passage the Stranger identifies and corrects certain confusions concerning the significance of negated predicates:

> *Str.* Whenever we speak of not being (so it seems), we don't speak of something contrary to being, but only different.
> *Tht.* How so?
> *Str.* For example, when we call something "not large," do you think we signify small by that expression any more than same-sized?
> *Tht.* No.
> *Str.* So, when it is said that a negative signifies a contrary, we shan't agree, but we'll allow only this much—the prefixed word "not" indicates something different than the words following the negative, or rather, different than the things which the words uttered after the negative apply to.
> *Tht.* Absolutely. (257b1–c4)[15]

The insight that is implicit throughout the discussion of negation is that the negation of a predicative proposition negates the predicate, i.e., the verb. The mistake that the Stranger identifies is that of supposing that the addition of "not" to a predicate yields an expression for the contrary of what is meant by the original predicate. Contraries are understood here as polar kinds or determinations within a family, such as hot-cold, young-old, or white-black. The Stranger illustrates this general point by noting that *not-larger (than Y)* doesn't mean *smaller (than . . .)* any more than it means *same-sized (as Y)*.

The analytical reading finds hints, in this passage, of a semantic analysis of negative predicates, one that is based on the relation of difference. This analysis is supposed to determine the sense of "not-*X*" on the basis of the

---

[15] The translation of this passage is Lesley Brown's. See "Negation and Not-being: Dark Matter in the Sophist," in *Presocratics and Plato: A Festschrift for Charles Kahn*, ed. A. Hermann (Las Vegas: Parmenides Publishing, 2001).

positive attribute expressed by *X* and the relation of difference between positive attributes. Thus, it purports to construe the predicative *is not* (*not to be*) in term of the *is* (*to be*).[16] It is a desideratum of any analytical interpretation that the truth, i.e., the truth-conditions, of a negative predication coincide with the falsehood, i.e., the falsity-conditions, of a positive predication.

In an essay on the *Sophist*, David Wiggins argues that all attempts to construe or make sense of the content of negated predicates lead to dead ends.[17] Wiggins proposes instead that affirmation and denial, thought of as two ways of applying a predicate to a subject, must be regarded as equally primitive notions. This conception of simple contradictory pairs is not presented as a reading of Plato's account in the *Sophist*, but as a competing account. Indeed, the negation sign, according to Plato, is attached to a predicate and thereby makes a new complete phrase, i.e., the Stranger emphasizes that the negated expression is one verb. Wiggins defends his account of negative predication as one that "can exploit everything that is clear about the theory of affirmative predication and completely displace Difference and the Other from the theory of Negation" (301–302).

We have already observed that the kind of account Wiggins proposes of the contradictory pair is inadequate. By interpreting the difference between affirmation and negation as a difference in propositional form, i.e., in the way predicate and subject are combined or related, we lose the internal unity of a contradictory pair—for such an account precludes us from seeing that affirmation occurs within negation: that "*S* is *F*" occurs within "*S* is

---

[16] This does not mean, according to the analytical interpretation, that the Stranger is proposing, for instance, that *not sitting* means *flying*, since sitting is a different attribute than flying; instead, according to these readers, this remark implicitly contains a quantifier. The two main rival analytical interpretations of negative predication correspond to the two analytical interpretations of the falsehood of simple propositions which we discussed earlier: the *Oxford interpretation* and the *incompatible range interpretation*. According to the *Oxford interpretation* the negation of a predicate X expresses a second-order attribute not-X that applies to something if all the attributes that apply to it are different from X; *difference*, on this interpretation, is simply the nonidentity of attributes. According to the *incompatible range interpretation*, *difference* is a relation between attributes expressed by predicates that belong to a range or family of incompossible predicates; and not-X is a second-order attribute that applies to something if there is an attribute Q, different from X (i.e., incompatible with it), that applies to it.

[17] "Sentence Meaning, Negation and Plato's Problem of Non-being," in *Plato: Modern Studies in Philosophy*, ed. G. Vlastos (London: Palgrave MacMillan, 1972).

not *F*." As such, this kind of account cannot capture the priority of affirmation and treats affirmation and negation symmetrically. By contrast, any account of contradictory pairs that treats the contradictory difference as a difference in predicative contents must regard the positive predicate as a semantically autonomous locus of truth or falsity concerning the subject (the predicate is something said truly or falsely about the subject). Such accounts ignore the dependence of positive predication on the unity of the contradictory pair. That is, they ignore the dominance of the contradictory pair over its positive member.

The analytical interpretation's construal of the sense of negative predicates, as well as Wiggins's account of negative predication as denial, are both attempts to identify the contradictory difference between simple pairs of propositions as a categorematic difference; I shall propose that, according to the teaching of the Stranger, this contradictory difference between a predicate and its negation is not categorematic.

McDowell, by contrast to the analytical readers, denies that there is a semantical thesis concerning the content of negative predicates in this passage (257b1–c4). More precisely, he claims that the only semantical thesis suggested by this passage is that

> "Not Beautiful" means exactly what it does, namely, *not beautiful;* the role of the notion of otherness [difference] is in an explanation, at a sub-semantical level, of why we do not need to fear that such a semantical remark is condemned to vacuity.[18]

According to McDowell, the notion of *difference* is not invoked by Plato as part of an analysis of the negated predicate, in the context of sub-semantical remarks concerning negative claims. Often, though not always, one can say that "*S* is not *F*" is true since "*S* is *G*" (e.g., this page is not white, since it is black instead). However, this remark is not meant to be part of the determination of the content of "not *F*." The possibility of such remarks belongs to the very grammar of negation, and McDowell takes it that all Plato does with his notion of *difference* is remind us of this grammar in order to correct the misunderstanding that a negation of a predicate has a determinate sense as a contrary relative to the original.

---

[18] McDowell, "Falsehood and Not-being in Plato's *Sophist*," 8.

McDowell's Stranger can be characterized as a *deflationist,* insofar as he seeks to remove Parmenidean difficulties by exposing the confusions about grammar from which they arise, instead of seeing in them a demand for an analysis:

> This unconcern with analysis need not seem a defect, if we see [the Stranger]'s project as what it is: not to give an account of the sense of phrases like "not beautiful," but rather to scotch a mistake about what entitles us to our confidence that they are not idle chatter, that they do indeed have the precise sense that we take them to have. (No need, in executing this project, to produce any substantive theory of what that sense is.) The mistake is worth scotching here, not for its own sake, but because if it is allowed to pass in this case it can be carried to undermine our confidence in the intelligibility of the "is not."[19]

McDowell argues that, through correcting a grammatical confusion about the use of negation, the Stranger in fact addresses and successfully removes the puzzle concerning falsity that goes back to an earlier characterization of falsehood which is given at 241a: "And a false proposition, I suppose, is to be regarded as stating of things that are, that they are not, and of things that are not that they are."

McDowell reads this characterization in terms of attributes, "bearing in mind the desirability of finding something to the point in 263b."[20] For example, "Theaetetus is in flight" represents *in flight,* which is not, as being. The Sophist must find this characterization of falsehood problematic, because he cannot see how "is not" can be anything but a synonym for "has the contrary of being" or "utterly is not." Therefore, it seems to him that we talk nonsense when we say that "Theaetetus is in flight" represents *in flight,* which is not (in relation to Theaetetus; though given the mistake which gets corrected by the Stranger's remarks in 257b1–c4, this qualification does not help), as being. Once this confusion concerning negation has been corrected, we can restate the formulation of falsehood that seemed problematic, avoiding the equation of "not-being" with: "opposite of being," or "in no way being."

---

[19] McDowell, "Falsehood and Not-being in Plato's *Sophist*," 7–8.
[20] McDowell, "Falsehood and Not-being in Plato's *Sophist*," 20.

(McDowell, the deflationist, tries to console the disappointed reader by assuring her that it is not a cost but a gain that we find in the *Sophist,* "not an unconvincing attempt on that interesting difficulty, but a wholly successful solution to a different one." He then continues with an afterthought: "It is true that we cannot easily find the different difficulty pressing," but "Parmenides would," he assures us.)

9.

Edward Lee proposed an interpretation of the Stranger's employment of *difference*, which he translates as Otherness,[21] that is distinct from the analytical and deflationist readings.[22] Lee focuses on the passage that concerns the partition of difference (257c–258c). I shall first outline Lee's interpretation of this passage, while pointing to certain weaknesses in it. I shall then build on Lee's insight, with the help of another of the Stranger's teachings in the *Sophist*, in order to give the correct reading of the Stranger's treatment of falsehood and negation.

In this passage Plato introduces what he calls "part of the nature of Otherness," asserting that that part of Otherness—and not simply Otherness itself—defines the non-being required to conclude the inquiry and trap the Sophist. Lee argues that the notion of Otherness that Plato employs in this passage is a new one which should be distinguished by its "logic" from the notion of Otherness that was hitherto in use in the dialogue. Indeed, he sees the important break in the dialogue as occurring at 257c5. Lee argues that this passage is not a continuation of the point concerning negation, large, small, and medium (257b1–c4) which, by contrast, McDowell considers to be the key to removing the confusion concerning negation which the Stranger addresses.

The passage itself is divided into three sections: first, in 257c5–d11, Plato presents his notion of "part of the nature of difference" by means of an analogy with the parts or branches of knowledge; second, in 257d12–258a10

---

[21] In discussing Lee's essay I shall adopt this translation.

[22] "Plato on Negation and Not-being in the *Sophist,*" *The Philosophical Review* 81, no. 3 (Jul. 1972): 267–304.

Plato argues that every such "part of Otherness" is, in its own way, as fully definite and no less real than any other form; and third, 258a11–c5, in which he concludes that non-being is, in its way, just as definite and no less real than being.

In the first section Plato introduces his notion of "part of the nature of Otherness" by means of an analogy with parts or branches of knowledge.[23]

Knowledge (episteme), according to Plato, is partitioned into parts that get their names from the specific field with which each is concerned. Lee paraphrases the Stranger's introduction of this partitioning as follows:

---

[23] 257c5:

> *Str.* And we should consider the following, if you agree.
>
> *Tht.* What?
>
> *Str.* It seems to me that the nature of the different is to be parcelled out, just like knowledge.
>
> *Tht.* How so?
>
> *Str.* Well, knowledge also is a single thing, surely, but each of its parts that applies to something is marked off and gets some special name of its own. That's why there are many skills and kinds of knowledge that get spoken of.
>
> *Tht.* Certainly.
>
> *Str.* And so with the nature of the different: though it's a single thing, it has parts in a similar fashion.
>
> *Tht.* Possibly, but shouldn't we say how?
>
> *Str.* Is there some part of the different that is set against the beautiful?
>
> *Tht.* There is.
>
> *Str.* So shall we say it's nameless, or that it has a name?
>
> *Tht.* That it has a name; because what—from time to time—we put into words as "not beautiful," it's this that is different from nothing other than the nature of the beautiful.
>
> *Str:* Now go ahead and tell me this.
>
> *Tht.* What?
>
> *Str:* Isn't it in the following way that the not beautiful turns out to be, namely, by being both marked off within one kind of those that are, and also set over against one of those that are?
>
> *Tht.* Yes.
>
> *Str.* Then it seems that the *not beautiful* is a sort of setting of being against being.
>
> *Tht.* That's absolutely right.
>
> *Str,* Well then according to this account, is *the beautiful* more a being than the not *beautiful?*
>
> *Tht.* Not at all.

The various areas or branches of knowledge get partitioned off from the un-differentiated general notion,[24] knowledge, and so come to have their various specific names, depending upon the special field with which, in each instance, the knowledge is concerned. Knowledge concerned with harmonies and rhythm is (let us say) what we call "music"; knowledge about letters and syntax (say) is "grammar"; knowledge about numbers, "arithmetic"; knowledge about woodworking, "carpentry"; and so forth. Knowledge is itself one general and unspecified notion, but each branch of it is marked off as a specific branch, and gets its specific name, according as it is directed to some specific subject matter (257cI o-d2). ("Plato on Negation and Not-being in the *Sophist*," 170)

Lee goes on to explain the analogy between the partitioning of knowl-edge and of Otherness by invoking a notion of the "directedness" of knowl-edge and of difference to specific beings:

According to Plato, the one general notion of Otherness gets "parceled out" or "apportioned" in just the same way as does knowledge. That is to say, then, Otherness too is "partitioned" as it is directed to various other specific be-ings. The notion of "Part of Otherness," just like that of a branch of knowledge, must thus be the notion of Otherness directed-to some specific being other than itself. It must be a determination of the notion of Otherness, via the specifying of that item otherness-than-which, which is, in that particular case, to be at issue. ("Plato on Negation and Not-being in the *Sophist*," 270–271)

Otherness is thus employed to elucidate the *negation sign;* the not-X is thus clarified by being rendered as "Otherness than X," or as "Otherness directed to X." This rendition shows, according to Lee, that not-X is not opposed to X as one kind or type to another, but as internally related to X. Thus, the use of "Otherness" reveals that a particular X and not-X are not opposed as a pair of contraries. More generally it reveals that "the relation of the not-X to the X does not hold, so to say, directly between the not-X and the X (as though they stood on quite the same level). The not-X is rather a construct, derived from the "X" (273).

---

[24] The characterization of knowledge *itself* as an "undifferentiated general notion" or as a "general and unspecified notion" is misleading, since it gives the impression that the Stranger takes *knowledge* to be a genus, with branches of *knowledge* as species marked by differentia. We shall see below that knowledge or difference in general cannot be regarded as forms in the same sense that the specific objects of knowledge are forms.

In drawing the analogy, the Stranger shifts the discussion to the form of the linguistic expressions for knowledge and negation. Lee, who notices this shift, writes: "In these lines Plato's exposition has moved (however transiently, as we shall see) into the formal mode and taken on an explicitly semantical air of concern with the sense of various linguistic expressions—expressions explicitly quoted and referred to as such, as linguistic items" ("Plato on Negation and Not-being in the *Sophist*," 274). Lee's use of the term "formal mode" here is misleading insofar as it suggests that the shift only concerns the manner of presentation. In fact, Plato's discussion of language and signification here is essential to his understanding of the internal relations that are the concern of the analogy. In fact, I would propose that what we have here is evidence that Plato recognizes that negative predication is the display, through an assertoric gesture, of the positive predication, inside the context of negation.

Lee describes the partition of difference and knowledge as "intensional determination" (p. 290), and contrasts such understanding of the partition with the extensionalist readings of the various analytical interpretations which, for example, seek to specify the content of not-X in terms of the relation between attribute X and other attributes.

The analogy between the partitioning of knowledge and the partitioning of Otherness, assimilates—in a way that is necessarily surprising from our contemporary perspective—the form of the object of knowledge with that of the object of negation.

Lee describes both knowledge and Otherness as "partitioned" through their being directed to specific beings, but he does not elucidate the general notion of directedness that applies both to knowledge and to Otherness/negation; instead he focuses on the directedness of Otherness.

At the heart of Lee's reading is a distinction between two senses or roles that Otherness takes in the dialogue. According to Lee, in a stretch of dialogue (251d–257a) which precedes the passage on the parts of Otherness and which discusses the structure of forms (that is, communion among forms[25]), *Otherness* plays a *supervening* role. That is, it obtains between self-standing, separable beings—the forms—that have their own nature

---

[25] The Stranger suggests that Otherness so pervades the world of forms that every form which is, is also (besides being itself) other than every other form. Since each form is "other than" every other form, it "is not" every other one of those forms. There was thus already a perfectly clear sense of "not-being" and "that which is not."

independently of being thus related. But in the doctrine of the Parts of Otherness it plays a role that Lee describes as *constitutive*:

> With the doctrine of the Parts of Otherness, he introduces a distinct and stronger notion of not-Being. Although non-Being here must still be analyzed in terms of otherness, that otherness now plays a different role. It no longer presupposes two separately given, separately distinct determinacies as relata (as in its supervenient role). Instead, it plays what I shall dub a constitutive role: Otherness itself, in conjunction with some *one* other term, now serves (as explained before) to constitute the being of a novel nature, the nature of a "Part of Otherness." Through this constitutive role, each Part of Otherness will be something whose whole nature consists in this: in otherness-than some other specified nature. It will therefore be something whose "nature" (thus, whose being) consists in its not-being-something-else. In its earlier, "supervenient" role, Otherness served to define non-beings which were also something in and of themselves, of their own proper nature. But its constitutive role—that is, the doctrine of the Parts of Otherness—defines a non-Being which is *not* also something in and of itself: a non-Being which has no proper nature "all its own," but whose being consists precisely and exclusively in its not being something else. And that fact, I submit, explains at last the fact with which this paper began: the fact that Plato twice remarks that it is the Part of Otherness, not Otherness just in itself, that answers his quest for an account of the real nature of non-being. Only in its constitutive role does Otherness define a notion which is, as Plato puts it (at 258e2–3), ὄντως τὸ μὴ ὄν: something which really and fully *is not*; a not-being that really does consist specifically and entirely in its NOT-being. ("Plato on Negation and Not-being in the *Sophist*," 286–287)

Lee would therefore agree with McDowell that "not beautiful" means exactly what it does, namely, *not beautiful,* since he is not trying to offer any analysis of not beautiful in terms of something which is semantically more basic than it. Plato, according to Lee, has not been trying to give a semantical analysis of negated predicates, nor has he in any sense "dissolved away" negation or "reduced it to" a (mere) partitioning of Otherness. But Lee's interpretation is not *deflationist.* I would like to instead suggest that Lee is attempting to give a *quietist* interpretation of the Stranger. By contrast to the deflationist, the quietist seeks to remove misunderstandings concerning the nature of the propositions or predicates that occur inside and outside negations (and other logical contexts) in a way that renders the principle of non-contradiction, and more generally the unity of the syllogisms of thinking and being, self-evident or truistic. The Stranger, according to Lee, is attempting, through the partition of Otherness, to determine the sense of a negative predicate on the basis of the sense of a positive predicate, in a way that elucidates their contradictory unity—the unity of a simple contradictory pair of predications.[26] But I will soon argue that Lee fails to outline a successful quietist position.

Lee's proposal is that the identification of the sense of not-*X* in terms of the constitutive notion of Otherness directed to *X* will solve the difficulty concerning the sense of negated predicates. For example, the sense of a predicate *is not-beautiful* is determinate as other than the beautiful; the being of the not-beautiful consists, thereby, precisely and exclusively in its not being beautiful. This also allows us to recognize the form of negative predication in a way that reveals the contradictory contrast of positive and negative predications. It reveals that the negative predication says the opposite of the positive:

> [W]e can now see clearly how the "constitutive" role of Otherness (that is, the doctrine of the Parts of Otherness) will deal with negative predication statements within these same requirements. What "x is not brown" says is that x (which is) partakes of a certain Part of Otherness (a Part which fully and securely *is,* as Plato takes such great pains to make clear at 257e2–258c3);

---

[26] Lee describes "partition" as an operation and associates it with Wittgenstein's notion of operation: "He [Plato] is holding instead—again very much like Wittgenstein—that negation is essentially an *operation:* it is the operation of partitioning Otherness. For that is the operation which constructs the sense of the negating statement from that of the very negated one—and so brings it about that the negating statement does negate precisely *that.* Plato's analysis of negation as the operation of partitioning Otherness thus serves to elucidate just why the sense of the negating statement does exclude that of the statement it negates, and why a statement and its negation cannot both of them be true (at the same time and in the same respects, and so forth). It explains these fundamental features of negation in that the very sense of the negation is seen to consist precisely *in* its exclusion of the sense negated; in its saying that that is what-is-not (or, equivalently, that what is is precisely otherness-than-that)" ("Plato on Negation and Not-being," 296–297). Lee's description of negation as "an operation which constructs the sense of the negating statement from that of the very negated one" shows that Lee fails to comprehend "operation" as inseparable from the full context principle. We shall see that this is his fundamental error.

it says that x partakes of that Part of Otherness whose "name" (257d9) is "(the) not-brown" and whose determinate nature consists in Otherness precisely-than-brown.[27]

10.

In a footnote to his essay on the *Sophist*, McDowell expresses dissatisfaction with Lee's notion of the constitutive role of Otherness:

> But Lee's "constitutive" role for otherness seems problematic. He explains it in remarks like this: "The determinate sense of 'x is not tall' . . . lies precisely, but lies entirely, in saying that tall is what x is not" (Lee, p. 295); but this would scarcely cut any ice with Parmenides.[28]

McDowell correctly detects a fundamental weakness in Lee's formulation. One gets the impression that the content of the negative predicate is constituted by a relation to a positive predicate which is given independently of it. In other words, we begin with a predicate that can by itself define a determinate region, and then invoke a certain intentional relation, e.g., Otherness, thereby getting a second, negative, predicate which applies precisely to anything that falls outside the extension of the first predicate. This kind of relational characterization turns up in Lee's attempt to gloss the content of the negated predicate:

> On this account, it is no part at all of the sense of the negating proposition that it should refer to any (much less to all) particular entities or predicates other than the negated predicate. The negating statement simply says that the subject partakes in the specific negative intention, Otherness than-the-predicate-negated. That is, it says that the subject's partaking lies outside the predicate negated; it does not say (on this account of it) that it lies in some other particular place outside that predicate (although that will no doubt be true), but just that it lies outside-that-predicate: anywhere-at-all but there.[29]

[27] Lee, "Plato on Negation and Not-being," 292.
[28] McDowell, "Falsehood and Not-being in Plato's *Sophist*," 8, fn11.
[29] Lee, "Plato on Negation and Not-being," 293.

The locution "anywhere-at-all but there" suggests a picture on which the extension of the positive predicate is determinate independently of the negated predicate, whereas the negated predicate is determinate in relation to it as "elsewhere." But McDowell correctly notes that this formulation does not address the Parmenidean worries concerning the sense of the negative predicate.

Since Lee apparently understands the positive predicate to be given prior to the negated predicate, he is open to the accusation that he does not take Otherness seriously as an explication of the internal constitutive unity of both positive and negative predications. The interpretation of negative predication that Lee ascribes to the Stranger acknowledges the priority of positive predication, but fails to recognize, *at one and the same time*, the dominance of the unity of the contradictory pair over each of its members.

11.

I want to propose that the invocation of knowledge in the account of negation does not appear merely for the sake of analogy. It will be useful to recall here a challenge that goes back to Parmenides's *Poem* and the Goddess's statement that being and thinking are the same. This should be read as stating that everything relevant to the truth of a judgment is already contained within judgment. The Goddess concludes on the basis of this point that negation and falsehood are unintelligible. But I wish to propose that, in fact, the difficulties concerning negation and falsehood are removed through the acknowledgment of the sameness of thinking and being. That is the upshot of §95 of Wittgenstein's *Philosophical Investigations*:

> "Thinking must be something unique." When we say, *mean*, that such-and-such is the case, then, with what we mean, we do not stop anywhere short of the fact, but mean: *such-and-such—is—so-and-so.*—But this paradox (which indeed has the form of truism) can also be expressed in this way: one can think what is not the case.

Note that in this passage Wittgenstein identifies the difficulties concerning negation as part of a single puzzle, one that is in no way distinct from the challenge of recognizing that the success or failure of a judgment / statement that something is the case does not depend on anything external to it. We can recognize that these paradoxes—paradoxes that have the form of truisms—are nothing other than the syllogisms of thinking and being. What is at issue throughout the passage is already present at the outset: that thinking must be something unique.[30] The passage suggests that, once the misunderstanding that obscures the self-evident character of these syllogisms is removed, the uniqueness of thinking will become apparent.

In order to liberate the truism from the seeming paradox that disguises it, we shall have to discover a perspective from which it is clear that the proposition p occurs in the same way within the context of indirect discourse, that is, in the ascription of judgment, and in the context of negation. We have to discover, that is, a perspective that grants us the revelatory point of view on the proposition that we have been looking for.

I will try to show that Lee's interpretation of the partition of difference and knowledge should be revised in light of an understanding of the sameness of form in knowledge and in the object of knowledge, namely, of the sameness of thinking and being, for which one can find evidence in the *Sophist*. The revised view of the partitions of knowledge and difference will allow us to understand the Stranger as a quietist who provides us with a view of the complexity of propositions that allows us to recognize the truth- and false-maker syllogisms, as truisms.

11.1. The Place of Activity within Being

In a stretch of the dialogue that precedes the initial presentation of the difficulties concerning non-being / what-is-not, and that leads to a constructive

---

[30] In *Mind and World*, McDowell quotes this remark, glossing it as follows:

> We can formulate this point in a style Wittgenstein would have be[en] uncomfortable with: there is no ontological gap between the sort of thing one can mean, or generally the sort of thing one can think, and the sort of thing that can be the case. When one thinks truly, what one think[s] is the case. So since the word is everything that is the case (as he himself once wrote), there is not [*sic*] gap between thought, as such, and the world. (p. 27)

But, given McDowell's Fregean notion of sense, he is not entitled to the truism on which he wishes to insist; he cannot recognize the truth-maker inference as valid. The Fregean notion of sense conceals the significance of the puzzle of negation to which Wittgenstein alludes, and which McDowell indeed almost ignores.

engagement with these difficulties, the Stranger turns his attention to the theme of *being,* which he recognizes as inseparable from, and as hard to clarify as, *non-being.* The Stranger begins by showing how the ancients were confused in their approaches to this theme. The discussion culminates in a debate which the Stranger stages between two competing contemporary positions. The competing factions in this debate, which the Stranger dubs *Gigantomachia,* are the materialists, who are cast in the role of giants, and the immaterialists (who are also called *friends of the forms*), who are cast in the role of "the gods."

The materialists he describes as dragging everything down to earth and as identifying being with body, with what is sensible and tangible, and so with coming-to-be or becoming *(genesis)*: that which varies over time. By contrast, the friends of the forms only confer the status of being on "certain intelligible and non-bodily forms" (246b7), and relegate the changing material things which the giants champion to the lower rank of becoming. Forms, according to the friends of the forms, exemplify being in the true sense insofar as they are not subject to change.

By inquiring whether a materialist can admit the being of the virtues of the soul, such as justice and intelligence, the Stranger comes to develop a more sophisticated materialism, according to which embodied capacities, to either affect the sensible character of things, or to be so affected, are *beings* (247c–248a).

By contrast, the friends of the forms sharply distinguish real being from coming-to-be, and consequently they also distinguish the perceptual capacity which deals with sensible qualities in perception from the soul which deals with forms in reasoning and knowledge:

> [B]y our bodies and through perception we have dealing with coming-to-be, but we deal with being by our souls and through reasoning. You say that being always stays the same and in the same state, but coming-to-be varies from one time to another. (248a)

The Stranger will show that the exclusion of activity from being, and thus from knowledge, renders knowledge unintelligible. I want to propose that the revised nonmaterialist conception of the soul, of the forms, and of knowledge as active, that all result from the Stranger's critique of the friends of the forms, is crucial for understanding the Stranger's partitioning of both difference and knowledge.

The Stranger isolates the two fundamental theses of the friends' doctrine concerning *real being* and shows that they are in fact incompatible with one another. The first thesis is that real being is changeless: it is always the same, and in the same respect. The second thesis is that real being is knowable—it is that which is dealt with in reasoning.

In addition to these two theses, the Stranger puts forward as uncontroversial a claim about the nature of knowledge: knowing is a case of acting (*poieîn*) in some way, and therefore being-known is a case of being acted upon (*paschein*). He then shows that the friends of the forms contradict themselves:

> [S]ince knowing is acting in some way, then necessarily that which is known must be acted upon. When being is known by knowledge according to this account, then insofar as it's known it's changed by having something done to it—which we say wouldn't happen to something that's at rest. (248d10–e4)

This conclusion contradicts the thesis that real being is inert, namely, that being always stays the same in the same respect; more generally, it contradicts the claim that a capacity and its activity do not belong to being.

The notion of forms as inert, abstract beings that are the locus of no life whatsoever—and are therefore extrinsic to the activity of the soul—renders knowledge and judgment unintelligible since it precludes us from recognizing the consciousness of judgment and knowledge as intrinsic to the soul.

In light of this difficulty the Stranger asks the following rhetorical question:

> Are we going to be convinced that change, life, soul, and thought have no place in *that which wholly is*, and that it never lives nor thinks, but always stays changeless, solemn and wholly devoid of intellect? (248e6–249a2)[31]

We are supposed to conclude that if knowledge and reason are intelligible, there must be a sense of *life,* and of *capacity, activity, change / rest* that have their home in being rather than in coming-to-be. The Stranger would reject

---

[31] In Ennead V.5.1, Plotinus invokes these lines in resistance to, among other things, the Stoic notion of *lekta* as contents external to the activity of *nous*. Since thinking cannot depend for its success on anything outside of it, Plotinus argues there that *nous* is what it knows, and consequently that the *noemata* must themselves be *nous*.

any conception of knowledge/judgment as a composite made up of, on the one hand, a subjective act of coming-to-be and, on the other hand, a form. For the same reason, he would reject any view according to which knowledge is an accident of a form and of the soul—for example, the view that, in knowledge, a form or a propositional content is externally related to the soul.[32]

As such, soul, knowledge, and form must be associated with a certain notion of activity in a way that will allow us to understand forms as immanent to the soul's activity, rather than external to it.

The Stranger emphasizes that *activity,* in the sense that has its home in being, cannot be assimilated to activity that has its home in coming-to-be, for any such assimilation denies the distinction between being and coming-to-be, and thus renders knowledge and reason unintelligible. (Putting this point in modern terminology, one could say that without the distinction between being and coming-to-be, one is forced into a form of psychologism concerning logical necessity.)

The Stranger argues, in fact, that a dissociation of being from coming-to-be, which is the view associated with the gods, and the assimilation of being and coming-to-be, which is the view associated with the giants, both lead to skepticism: the denial of knowledge (249c2–5). According to the Stranger, it is the business of the philosopher, who values reason and knowledge, to fight with every argument at his disposal against those who, while doing away with knowledge, intelligence, or reason, continue to make assertions, for they contradict themselves and are thus subject to refutation (249c5–8).

But in order to render knowledge intelligible, the philosopher will have to go beyond the dilemma concerning the forms, i.e., real being: "He has to be like a child begging for 'both' and say that *which is*—everything—is both unchanging and that which changes."

---

[32] In his "Plato's Paradox that the Immutable is Unknowable" (*Philosophical Quarterly*, Vol. 19, No. 74, 1969), David Keyt calls the following Plato's paradox: on the one hand, a form, since it is an object of knowledge, must be completely changeless; on the other hand, in coming to be known, it must undergo change. He argues that this paradox is removed once we see that coming to be known is an accidental change of the form. In a footnote he associates this move with the Platonism of Frege (p. 14). But, as we have seen, a construal of judgment or knowledge as a relation between a thinker and content is hopelessly incoherent.

But how can a form be both changing and unchanging? Or, equivalently, how can the form in knowledge be the same and different than the form which is the object of knowledge?

The answer lies in the notion of the syncategorematic form or capacity that we have introduced in this work. The same form is in both knowledge and the object of knowledge. The notion of a syncategorematic form allows philosophers to hold onto that which is—being—in *both* ways, as "both unchanging and that which changes." The change that the syncategorematic form . . . *beauty* undergoes in informing the judgment / knowledge that Helen is beautiful is a change in activity in a syncategorematic sense. This change, which is not a change, is manifested by the difference between the judgment "Helen is beautiful," and the judgment "*A* judges Helen is beautiful."[33,34] The idea of syncategorematic form only emerges later in the dialogue, in the discussion of the partition of knowledge and of Otherness (257c–258c); it is only there that the philosophers who begged for both are granted their wish. Essential to understanding the notion of syncategorematic form is seeing that the partition of knowledge is brought together in the dialogue together with the partition of Otherness, and not just for the sake of the analogy but as two interrelated parts of a complete account of the logical unity of thinking and being. As we have remarked, to recognize the validity of the syllogisms of thinking and being, we must come to see that the very same proposition occurs both when it is negated and when it is ascribed as a judgment: namely, in not-*p* and in *A judges that p*. This perspective is attained by combining the lessons of the partition of knowledge and the partition of Otherness.

11.2.

We are now in a position to reread the discussion of the partition of knowledge. The lesson we can draw from the discussion of knowledge of the forms (248d–e) is that knowledge is partitioned into parts or branches by the forms

---

[33] The difference is manifested by the fact that (*p* or not-*p*) is a tautology, whereas (A thinks *p* or A thinks not-*p*) is not.

[34] The view that the form in knowledge or in thinking is the same as the form in being will be familiar to readers of Aristotle. In the case of intellectual knowledge *(nous, nouesis),* Aristotle holds that, in being known, the form of the object comes to be in the rational soul.

of their respective objects, and that each part has the same form as its object. The form that is common to a part of knowledge, a special science, or to a judgment and its respective object, is a syncategorematic form. Thus, the form which is active in knowledge / judgment is the same as the form of the object of knowledge, i.e., a fact. For example, the knowledge of biology has the same form as that which is inherent in facts concerning biology.

According to Plato, knowledge is, as we have seen, partitioned into parts that get their names from the form with which each is concerned. The partition of knowledge is not of genus into species, and therefore the role of the complement X in 'knowledge of X' is not to introduce a specific differentia of a genus. The dependence of knowledge of X on X is constitutive, and the discussion of knowledge of forms (248d–e) suggests that knowledge of X has the same form as X. The X in question (e.g., grammar) indicates the syncategorematic form of the special knowledge of a certain region of facts (e.g., grammatical knowledge), and it is also the form of the objects of such knowledge, namely, of the facts that lie in this region (grammatical facts). It appears therefore that 'Knowledge of___' is an operation in the sense that was introduced in Chapter 1, and that the complement therefore plays the role of displaying a logical form as the basis for the operation.

In light of the analogy between the partition of Otherness and the partition of knowledge, we can make the same point about Otherness and negation. The same syncategorematic or logical form is active in the fact that Helen is beautiful, and in the fact that Quasimodo is not beautiful. Thus, Plato is conveying, by the analogy between difference and knowledge, that the beautiful and the not beautiful are distinguished as two activities of the same logical form: __is *beautiful,* and that this distinction is syncategorematic.

Lee's reading of the dialogue remains incomplete and vulnerable to McDowell's objection because he fails to associate the distinction between the supervenient and constitutive roles of Otherness with two senses of form. What we should say is that, in its supervening role, Otherness holds between categorematic forms, whereas in its constitutive role Otherness is an operation that displays the dependence of one act of a syncategorematic form on another. Lee fails to note that Otherness (or knowledge) is not partitioned in virtue of being directed to a categorematic form, but rather on the basis of the act of a syncategorematic form.

A verb (predicate) in a simple predicative proposition is associated with a form in two senses: one categorematic and one syncategorematic (we can also say that it is associated with two forms). The categorematic form is a determination or attribute that is signified by the verb, whereas the syncategorematic form is a two-way logical capacity whose positive and negative acts are contradictory. The form in the categorematic sense is prior, for it is associated with the positive predication, whereas the form in the syncategorematic sense dominates the categorematic form, for it is associated with the unity of the contradictory pair.

For example, the syncategorematic form __is *beautiful* is active in the positive judgment "Helen is beautiful," and in the negative judgment "Quasimodo is not beautiful"—but also in the positive fact that Helen is beautiful, and the negative fact that Quasimodo is not beautiful. This form should be distinguished from the categorematic form—the attribute *beauty*—which Venus and Helen share but which Quasimodo lacks. The reality of beauty as a categorematic form lies in the positive fact. However, the unity which constitutes the being of a simple judgment or a fact, whether positive or negative, is the syncategormatic form. The two acts of the syncategorematic form are therefore the veridical being and non-being[35] (. . . is the case / true; . . . is not the case / true) of the veridical being, which is the syncategormatic form.

The reality of beauty as a categorematic form lies in the positive fact. However, the unity which constitutes the being of a simple judgment or a fact, whether positive or negative, is the syncategormatic form. The acts of the syncategorematic form—assertions and facts—are therefore the veridical being and non-being (. . . is the case / true, . . . is not the case / true) of the veridical being which is the syncategormatic form. Consequently, the predicate expression ". . . beautiful" displays, in all its occurrences, the veridical being of the being which is the syncategorematic form: __ is beautiful. The display can be self-identifying, and thus an assertion that the veridical being is. But within the context of negation (e.g., the "Quasimodo is not beautiful") ". . . beautiful" is a mere display of the veridical being, one that is in service of asserting that it is not.

---

[35] I propose that the general forms of being and non-being that the Stranger invokes in the discussion of the partition of difference are the two acts of the syncategorematic form, which is associated with the predicative unity as such. The veridical form of being is displayed by each positive predicative proposition.

We are now equipped to resolve the apparent contradiction between Plato's position in the *Sophist*, namely, that the not-beautiful has no less being than the beautiful itself, and his position in the *Statesman* that denies the existence of the negative form. The form discussed in the *Statesman* is a categorematic form—it is a determination, a predicative reality, whereas the point concerning beautiful and not-beautiful pertains to syncategorematic form. The not-beautiful has no less being then the beautiful itself, since both are acts of the same veridical being, i.e., the syncategorematic form__is beautiful.

11.3.

I have arranged the four logical activities of the one form in Table 3.1.

We can use this table to interpret the Stranger's characterization in 263 of the truth and falsehood of the simplest *logoi*:

(I) The true one says of a thing that is about you [Theaetetus] that it is. (II) The false one says a different thing from the thing that is; that is (III) it says, of a thing that is not, that it is.

So the true proposition *Theaetetus is sitting* says of the syncategorematic form *Sitting*, which is about *Theaetetus*, that it is about Theaetetus. The same form, viz.,__is *sitting*, is active positively both in the fact and in the judgment concerning Theaetetus. The proposition "Theaetetus is flying" is false, since one form,__is *flying*, is active positively in the judgment "Theaetetus is flying," but negatively in the fact *Theaetetus is not flying*. In other words, in the case of falsehood, the syncategorematic form is active in opposite ways in the judgment and in the corresponding fact.[36]

Table 3.1

Form: Beautiful	Positive (a veridical being)	Negative (a part of difference)
In the soul	Judgment: s is beautiful	Judgment: s is not beautiful
In the world (beings)	State of affairs: *s is beautiful*	State of affairs: *s is not beautiful*

[36] Chapter 7 of Aristotle's *Metaphysics* Gamma is devoted to the logical principle of the excluded middle, which is stated at the opening of the chapter:

This understanding of the internal unity of positive and negative predications removes the deep puzzle concerning falsehood, and it should
be obvious that it also removes the mystery of negation, as well as the
problem of the sense of negative expressions. Moreover, it is easy to see
that the *apophantik* conception of truth and falsehood, which is based on
this understanding of the activity of the form, allows us to lift the air of
paradox and to see the truth- and falsity-maker syllogisms as effectively
truisms.

> Nor, on the other hand, is it possible that there should be anything in the middle of a
> contradiction, but it is necessary either to assert or to deny any one thing of one thing.
> (1011b23)

The last line should not be read as the ridiculous claim that one must have an opinion
about everything, or a ready answer to any question, but rather that one asserts either
by affirming or by denying something of something, and thus there is no third truth-
assessable act, placed in the middle of these, that is incompossible with both affirmation and denial.

To reveal that this point is in fact self-evident, Aristotle gives a definition of truth
and falsehood:

> This will be plain if we first define what truth and falsehood are: for to say that that which
> is not or that which is not is, is a falsehood; and to say that that which is is and that which
> is not is not, is true. (1011b26–29)

The key to understanding this definition is that copula "to be" is used here in the
veridical sense of "to be true" / "is the case," and yet is not external to the predicative
unity of that which is or is not the case, namely, the veridical being. The definition
must accordingly be read as an expression of the *apophantic* account of truth. It reveals
that the context of truth and falsehood and of judgment / assertion is a veridical being
which is a two-way syncategormatic capacity. Assertion, namely, saying that something
is and saying that something is not, are the two possible acts of a veridical being; so are
the truth conditions of these assertions: something being the case, and something not-
being the case.

From here we can quickly conclude that there is no place for a truth-assessable act
placed between affirmation and negation: the truth of this middle would constitute the
falsehood of *both* affirmation and negation—yet Aristotle's definition reveals that the
truth / falsehood of affirmation is the same as the falsehood / truth of negation.

In the subsequent passage of chapter 7, Aristotle notices that, in fact, the illusion
that there is a middle thing between the contradictory being the case and not being the
case rests on confusing the negative predicate with a contrary, the confusion the
Stranger identifies and corrects in the *Sophist* (257b1–c4).

11.4. Metaphysics as Quietism

We have described the Stranger's approach to the Parmenidean puzzles as quietist, and contrasted it with the analytical and deflationist approaches. Quietism does not seek to reduce not-being to being through an analysis of negation and truth- and falsity conditions, or to show that the point of view from which the use of negation appears unintelligible rests merely on a confusion about the actual use of words. Instead, the quietist seeks to render the unity of thinking and being (and non-being) self-evident by attaining clarity concerning the way logical unity is revealed through the occurrence of propositions or predicates inside and outside negations and other logical contexts.

I want to suggest that we can come to recognize that metaphysics—correctly understood—is quietism, by learning, from within quietism, how to read the "meta-" of the "metaphysics." The lesson of quietism is that "meta-" does not point toward a science that comes "after" the physics, nor does it point toward supernatural entities such as divine substances, or a region of facts that lie "beyond" or "over and above" nature.

Instead, we can conclude from quietism that the "meta-" is the beyond of the syncategorematic relative to the categorematic; in particular, it is the syncategorematic unity of simple contradictory pairs, the unity of determination and the nothing (or Otherness) of determination, which dominates the positive members of the pair. The philosophical logic that removes the Parmenidean puzzles and renders apparent the truistic unity of thinking and being must therefore be, in this sense, metaphysical.

Acknowledgments

In writing this book I was fortunate to enjoy the deep friendship, assistance, and involvement of Jonathan Lear, Jim Conant, Ian Blecher, Michael Thompson, and Robert Pippin.

I was assisted by the kindness and generosity of many others; it would be ridiculous for me to try to name all of them, but I often count their names in my heart.

I am grateful to Lindsay Waters of Harvard University Press for his patience and his belief in this project.

I wish to dedicate this book to the memory of my father and mother, Joshua (Shika) and Ada (Adi) Kimhi.

Index